HOW TO SOLVE STUDENT ADJUSTMENT PROBLEMS

A Step-by-Step Guide
for Teachers and Counselors

JONATHAN PORTER SMITH

**THE CENTER FOR APPLIED
RESEARCH IN EDUCATION**
West Nyack, New York 10995

**To my wife Pat and my family—
Anne, Jim, Adam, Jeremy, and Eliza**

Library of Congress Cataloging-in-Publication Data

Smith, Jonathan Porter.
    How to solve student adjustment problems : a step-by-step guide
for teachers and counselors / Jonathan Porter Smith.

    p.   cm.
    Includes bibliographical references.
    ISBN 0-87628-415-2
    1. Student adjustment.   I. Title.
LB1139.S88S63   1990   89-77472
371.93—dc20   CIP

ISBN 0-87628-415-2

**THE CENTER FOR APPLIED
RESEARCH IN EDUCATION**
BUSINESS & PROFESSIONAL DIVISION
A division of Simon & Schuster
West Nyack, New York 10995

PRINTED IN THE UNITED STATES OF AMERICA

About the Author

J. Porter Smith is a certified guidance counselor, social studies teacher, and teacher of children with moderate special needs. For the last 20 years he has worked with middle and secondary school students with moderate to severe school adjustment problems. As the director of a public school therapeutic day program, he has developed a clinical education model that combines treatment techniques from the fields of education and child and family therapy.

Mr. Smith is employed at present as a dean of students and works with teachers and parents on early identification and treatment of student adjustment problems. He also owns an educational consulting business and provides both in-service training and computerization services to schools. He has worked as a consultant for the University of Massachusetts, the American Speech and Hearing Association, and many public schools.

Mr. Smith received both his Bachelor's degree in Psychology and his Master's degree in Guidance and Psychological Services from Springfield College in Springfield, Massachusetts. He is a member of the Massachusetts Teachers Association, the National Teachers Association, the Council for Exceptional Children, and the American Association for Counseling and Development.

About This Resource

How to Solve Student Adjustment Problems is a guide to identifying and treating students with school adjustment problems. It gives you concrete examples of steps to take along the way, from defining the problem, setting goals, and initiating contact with the student and parents to setting up behavior contracts and monitoring systems, and, if necessary, organizing special teams of teachers, parents, and professionals. It alerts you to the possibilities for failure at each step and how to avoid them. Perhaps most usefully, it shows you how to work constructively with parents, even those who come in blaming the school and those who never seem to come in. It tells you what steps to take *before* a referral for special education services and explains what to expect *after* referral, including how to advocate for students. Finally, it focuses on three particularly troublesome topics for contemporary educators: substance abuse and addiction; child abuse and neglect; and attention deficit hyperactivity disorder and its treatment.

Part One, The Call For Help, presents the various ways problems come to our attention. It discusses the signs that indicate students are having adjustment problems and provides descriptions of eight types of serious school adjustment problems. If any of your students fits one of these eight descriptions, you are probably already struggling to find some way to help him or her. Part One provides answers to these questions:

- What is the role of stress in producing school problems?
- How do I know if I am dealing with a student who has a serious adjustment problem?
- What symptoms should alarm me, and where do I turn for help?

Part Two, Tools for Change, introduces techniques for helping students to change their unproductive behavior, including tools for identifying and sorting problem behaviors, behavior management programs, contracts, and monitoring sheets. Classroom teachers and counselors can use them to begin helping students right away. While many students will show immediate improvements, others will not; Part Two also leads you through a process of screening and evaluation that will help you to decide when to refer the student to special sevices.

As you try to help a student in your classroom and find that nothing seems to work, you begin to realize that you are dealing with a serious adjustment problem. Part Three, Teamwork, discusses ways to expand your efforts to help the student, by engaging parents and using the specialists in your school and/or community. Many programs to help students fail because of conflicts between the school and parents. Few students can be helped with their adjustment problems if their parents do not believe in what you are doing. Specific techniques are presented in Chapter Seven to help you understand and cope with parents who seem to want to fight you. Specifically, Part Three will help you to:

- Draw an angry or reticent parent onto your team.
- Conduct a structured family-school meeting.
- Develop simple and realistic approaches to help your students to adjust to school.
- Understand the roles of a large number of support people in the schools and community, who are described in a "Who's Who" of public school and community agency professionals.

Part Four, Special Education, is a survival kit for the teacher or counselor dealing with special education. It will help you to navigate the maze of procedures and services that you may face and answers the following questions:

- Who qualifies for special education?
- How do I prepare a parent for the IEP process?
- What can I expect as a member of the special education team?
- What do I do if I am asked to change my teaching approach to accommodate a special needs child, but do not have the time or materials to do so?

Part Four also offers guidelines for writing educational plans and developing special education programs for students with social or emotional adjustment problems.

Part Five, Special Topics, addresses three difficult issues currently of great concern to educators: helping students who have substance abuse or addiction problems, recognizing and dealing with child abuse and neglect, and accommodating to the frustrating and often controversial task of educating students who exhibit attention deficit hyperactivity disorder.

Finally, an appendix helps you to help parents find a therapist in the community, and a final appendix offers the theoretical background for the techniques for resolving conflict introduced in the book.

How to Solve Student Adjustment Problems is a practitioner's handbook. You may have 125 students in your classes but spend a majority of your time and energy on just the few who have adjustment problems. These students will pressure you into responding to them in atypical ways until they get help. In many cases, so will their families. With this book, you'll be able to take positive steps to help these students, without sacrificing the education of the rest.

J. Porter Smith

Acknowledgments

The author wishes to express his gratitude to the following people for supporting this project and/or providing editorial assistance:

In particular, to Patricia, Anne, and Wilbert Smith, who, as members of my family, kept my spirits up and my energy flowing; and to F. Alexander Blount, Ed.D., who helped to inspire me to find better ways to help students and their families.

And to The Amherst-Pelham (Mass.) Regional School District and the faculty of Amherst-Pelham Regional Junior High School: Linda Sears, Billie Howes, Sy Friedman, Jeanne Kamansky, John Burruto, Margo Barnhart, Ron Bell, Ed.D., Keith King, Dennis Rosen, M.D., Joel Herskowitz, M.D., Michael Stein, M.D., William Mathews, Ph.D., Jane Lyons, David Sprague, M.S.W., Barbara Sprague, M.S.W., Pat Schumm Rosen, Ed.D., Tina Lalonde, Mary Seppala, Siv Sandberg, Sharon Howard, Robert F. Murphy, and Wendy Kohler.

Contents

PART V SPECIAL TOPICS

Part I

THE CALL
FOR HELP

1

How Students Call for Help

Students in every classroom in every school have adjustment problems. Some problems disappear in time, and others do not require help from adults. School problems are not adjustment problems unless they significantly interfere with the education and welfare of the student. The challenge we face as educators is to determine when a student has an adjustment problem and when we must do something to try to help. Obviously teachers and counselors cannot respond to every little deviation from normal behavior. Otherwise, all our energy would be consumed by chasing false leads. We must focus our energy on students who need our intervention. But there is also a pitfall in ignoring too much. Student adjustment problems that are allowed to fester become more serious from year to year. Eventually, many of them become so serious that, for students above the ninth grade, they are almost impossible to treat.

When should we act? This is the question faced by all educators concerned with the well-being of their students.

We should take action when we see signs of stress. However, our actions must be in proportion to the degrees of severity of the problem. We *do not* call the psychiatrist when the student forgets his or her pencil for the first time. We *do* tell the school principal when the student is absent from class without an excuse for the twentieth time.

This chapter discusses how students tell us when they need help and how much help they need. It provides a way to deal with the dilemma of whether to do something. It answers the question, "Does this student have a significant adjustment problem?"

STRESS PRODUCES SYMPTOMS

When students have problems, they experience stress. It is not always easy or necessary for teachers or counselors to know specifically what these problems are to know that you are detecting signs of stress.

Students display their distress by producing signs or symptoms. Their stress may be indicated by any of thousands of possible signs, but some common examples are the following: avoiding tasks, disobeying adults, arguing, looking upset or unhappy, and feeling ill. As teachers, you frequently have an intuitive sense of when a student is in distress. It is important to trust that intuition and to realize that when a student has presented you a signal it is time to take notice and to provide help.

SYMPTOMS REFOCUS US

Students have unique ways of distracting us from our daily routines and refocusing us on their behavior. There are times when this refocusing is normal and appropriate and times when it is not.

> All teachers want their students to ask questions at appropriate times. But if a student feels compelled to ask the same question repeatedly and refuses to proceed with an assignment, it may indicate that there is a more serious problem.

Symptoms that are significant enough to make teachers notice them play a critical role in the process of a student's adjustment to stress. Students who cannot distract you from what you are doing are left with no other option but to develop a more powerful source of distraction, usually more serious or persistent symptoms. This will force you to focus on their behavior.

> Harold blurts out some inappropriate comment in math class without raising his hand. His teacher ignores him; Harold blurts out slightly louder; the teacher glances at Harold and warns him to stop; Harold blurts out and pokes Sally; the teacher stops the lecture and tells Harold to go to the office.

Anyone who hears Harold's behavior in math class could conclude that he is obnoxious, and they may be right! But most of us know that simply calling Harold "obnoxious" is no diagnosis. While we may experience him that way, before we can help him, and consequently improve the atmosphere of the classroom, more has to be done. It is important to determine what symptoms do to arouse a response from teachers or parents.

Conscious Symptoms

Some students who need to attract your attention for the purpose of getting assistance can ask you directly for that help. When that happens, producing a symptom is not necessary. The direct communication between adult and student has been effective in getting the adult to attend to the stressful situation. But at other times, even if students know what they want, they cannot find a way to articulate their needs to a teacher or counselor. At such times, producing a symptom will serve the purpose of calling for help.

> Johnny knows that if his science notebook is not up to date each Friday, Mr. Scibelli will ask him to stay after school the following Tuesday. This is an established classroom policy. Johnny may be lazy, or he may be disorganized and in need of extra help. It is difficult to tell the difference. He knows that he will be told to come in after school if his notes are not complete. In this way he is guaranteed of getting extra help even if going for help voluntarily is difficult for him. Maybe

he has been telling himself that he has to go to a tutorial after school, but has been procrastinating or is uncomfortable with approaching the teacher. He finds a simple solution: leave several items out of this week's notes and reliable Mr. Scibelli will extend an invitation to come after school next Tuesday. Johnny knows he needs help and has an easy device for getting the teacher to provide it.

His symptom, poor notes, triggers a response from an adult to change things. Johnny has done this in a conscious and fairly responsible manner, even though he couldn't take the initiative to go for extra help on his own.

Unconscious Symptoms

Students can also initiate the cry for help in ways of which they are unaware. From the time they are very small, they take in and store information about the ways in which the adults react to stress. Through thousands and thousands of observations, most of which are made unconsciously, students begin to develop a capacity to predict a response to patterns they have observed. They consequently may act in ways that will arouse adult responses without knowing they are doing so or being aware of what the response will be. Their behaviors are an unconscious triggering mechanism that asks the adult to provide help.

> Suzy learned when she was an infant that fussing got her mother's attention. Her mother was very responsive and appeared delighted to care for and nurture Suzy. As Suzy went through early childhood, she began to notice that at times her mother looked unhappy and withdrawn. Without being aware of it, Suzy became concerned about her mother. Quite accidentally, she also noticed that when she cried or became upset, her mother stopped looking withdrawn and unhappy and rushed over to soothe and care for her. An unconscious pattern formed in which Suzy began to predict that her fussing would make her mother appear to be happier. The relationship between Suzy's being upset and mother's coming to help and then looking happier continued through adolescence. Suzy learned that her mother looked better emotionally when she was able to play the role of a parent who was helping, nurturing, and soothing her children.

In seventh grade geography class Suzy's teacher, Ms. Jones occasionally comes to school looking a little withdrawn and depressed. On these days Suzy finds herself chatting with her classmate in social studies. This has never been a problem in other classes. After several warnings from her teacher, Suzy finally receives a detention, which is highly unusual for her. Her talking in social studies may have occurred because of Suzy's unconscious habit of attracting the attention of someone who looks depressed or unhappy.

These two examples represent the manner in which students *may* use symptoms both consciously and unconsciously to trigger reactions from adults. The rest of this book is written with the assumption that student's symptoms play a vital purpose in alerting the surrounding social system when problems exist. This premise can be applied to a wide range of student and adolescent adjustment problems. Healthy students in well-adjusted families have both conscious and unconscious devices that can work effectively to get adults to help them. But other students may find themselves frustrated in their attempts to attract help, and, therefore, they are forced to develop serious symptoms. Unfortunately, some students must commit crimes before they can trigger adults to help them, even if this means attracting the attention of the local court system to take charge of their lives.

The symptoms of our students will relentlessly push us to provide safe boundaries for them.

SYMPTOMS THAT SHOULD ALARM US

One of the hardest things you must do is to decide whether or not to take some kind of action when you detect a behavior that might be a serious problem. Some problems are minor and pass in time without your doing anything. Others require modest actions from us, and still others demand a great amount of time, commitment, and energy. Knowing how a *serious* adjustment problem might appear can help you to be aware of what to look for.

The descriptive sketches that follow are an introduction to the subject of serious school adjustment problems. Each description is a composite of behaviors that may represent several kinds of problems to psychologists. The list is not intended to represent every type of problem. It answers the questions, "How do you know if you are dealing with a student with a social or emotional problem?" or "How might a student with a problem appear to the parent or teacher?"

Any student whose behavior matches one or more of the following descriptions has a problem adjusting to school. The severity of a problem can vary somewhat, depending upon whether or not the student is in any immediate danger and how resistant he or she is to receiving help from adults. Counselors and teachers can survey the following series of behavioral sketches. They will increase your awareness of behavioral patterns that usually indicate that a student is struggling in school and requires further evaluation.

Poor Social Adjustment

Students who continually experience conflicts with their peers or who appear to have little or no peer contact have a social adjustment problem. Social problems limit the student, so he or she is unable to derive a normal amount of social and academic benefit from being in school. These students may be characterized as having frequent peer conflicts and are unable to use the resources of the administration, guidance, and/or teaching staff to learn how to resolve their problems. In other cases they may appear to be socially isolated and unable to make friends. They avoid group activities, after-school events and isolate themselves in the halls. When asked what they think about the other students in school, students with social adjustment problems may either give no opinion or claim that no one else in school is friendly. They have not learned how to explore and to build positive relationships with other students.

Impulsivity

Impulsive students frequently seem well intentioned, but are unable to control their behaviors and follow established classroom and school procedures. They may be students who have learning disabilities or problems focusing on classroom activities. They also may have emotional problems that prevent them from concentrating in class. Typically, these students have an inability to control an impulse to act before thinking. Consequently, they are often inadvertently disruptive and frequently unable to respond to supervision. Parents find these students disorganized, easily frustrated, and frequently unable to explain what the teacher expects of them. Teachers find these students to be distractible, overactive, unable to follow directions, and inconsistent in their academic achievement. One day they may perform very well; the next day they appear to have forgotten what they have learned.

Passive-Aggressive Behavioral Styles

Passive-aggressive students deal with their stressful feelings through withdrawal or avoidance. These students do not do assignments and fail to respond to extra help. They fail to keep appointments, lose monitoring sheets, and feign ignorance when asked if they know how to complete a task. There is a tendency for teachers to feel that the more energy they put into helping this type of student, the less the student does. It is easy to believe that a passive-aggressive student is really just lazy. Both teachers and counselors find these students elusive. They seem to have a talent for dodging responsibility while remaining courteous and friendly. Many passive-aggressive students have a well-developed battery of excuses and rationalizations for not being able to fulfill their school or family responsibilities. These excuses are not usually a cover for laziness, but a cover for serious emotional problems, problems that teachers can easily overlook.

Manipulative Personality

Manipulative students are often disruptive and provocative. They absorb an inordinate amount of staff time because they skip classes, lie about their whereabouts, and distort interactions with adults and students. It is extremely difficult to isolate one behavior on which to focus because these students create such an array of issues and problems. It is extremely difficult to diagnose the real problem. As soon as the parent or teacher attempts to intervene on one problem, these students present several other problems. A primary characteristic of a manipulative student is his or her talent for finding ways to engage adults in negative ways. They are masters at arguing about whether or not they have been dealt with fairly and are skilled at finding ways to force adults to continue to interact with them. Some adults find that the act of disciplining them can feel like rewarding them.

Hostile, Acting-Out Behavioral Style

Students who have unresolved anger about themselves and other people fall into this category. They abuse other students verbally and physically and frequently abuse teachers verbally. They overreact to adult intervention by becoming incensed when disciplined. Unless they are closely supervised, they say and do cruel things to other students. They require constant supervision to ensure that the rights of other students are protected. Hostile students are easy to identify because their behaviors demand immediate adult attention. They attract the attention of teachers and parents through negative behaviors and seem to have a talent for getting caught.

Anxious or Depressed Affect

Some students have psychological problems that cause them to be depressed, withdrawn, and/or nervous in school. Efforts by adults to help them may be graciously received by the student, but nevertheless they remain unable to respond to that help. These students often want to please teachers, but serious levels of emotional disturbance prevent them from doing so.

Anxious students experience unusual amounts of fear and discomfort when faced with challenging tasks, such as taking a test or preparing an essay. This anxiety distracts them from focusing on the assigned task and may contribute to avoidance behaviors such as losing assignments or becoming overly dependent on adult assistance.

Depressed students appear to have no energy. They seem content to sit quietly in the back of the room and do not seem to worry about doing poorly. Frequently, they are tardy or absent from school. They may appear tired, withdrawn, and socially isolated. Depression is frequently an underlying cause for many of the other adjustment problems.

Antisocial Personality

Antisocial students represent the extreme form of several other groups just described. The primary difference lies in their inability to demonstrate appropriate moral judgment. They are unable to discriminate between right and wrong, and they may be dangerous. They may commit crimes or hurt people with no apparent remorse. It is not uncommon for these students to be intelligent and to have good social skills, although they usually underachieve in school. They are in some cases very charming, but periodically will disrupt the school. Rarely do these students show positive behavior changes in response to discipline or psychological intervention. Antisocial students can present themselves well to adults if they believe these adults are observing them. When they make the mistake of allowing themselves to be caught committing an antisocial act, they are skilled at convincing adults that what happened was "just a misunderstanding and will never happen again." Unfortunately, these students do not appear to be able to learn from past experience. They may not be able to comprehend fully the fact that they have caused other people harm and, therefore, do not feel compelled to change their behavior.

Phobic Reactions

Phobic students have serious psychological problems that apparently prevent them from attending school. When they refuse to attend school, they report to adults a variety of reasons or excuses. These reasons may include fear of riding the bus or passing in the halls, fear of speaking out in class or taking tests, fear of changing clothes in the locker room, fear of other students ridiculing or making fun of them, and fear of being hurt physically by other students. Students who refuse to go to school for these reasons usually have serious adjustment problems with many different possible underlying causes. It is common for these causes to be other than the ones the student reports. Therefore, teachers should be cautious about focusing solely on the problem the student reports. Thorough psychological and family evaluations usually uncover additional problems that require treatment before the student can be successful in school. (Note: Many students report fears to their teachers or parents. These must be dealt with as legitimate concerns. However, if a student is refusing to attend school more than 20 percent of the time due to these fears, the student may have a serious adjustment problem.)

You should not consider the eight composites presented as rigid and exclusive categories. They are descriptive sketches representing a wide range of the behaviors for which students need help. A student's adjustment problem may cross several of these descriptive groups. If you believe a student has an adjustment problem, the chances are you are correct. The use of a team is an effective approach to learn more about a problem. The school psychologist and/or consulting psychological consultant are excellent resources for parents or teachers who have questions about a student's behavior and general level of adjustment to school.

The behaviors described are the "red flags" counselors and teachers need to watch for. If one is spotted, it is time to investigate further.

2

Identifying Problems

Chapter Two will help you to identify and work on a wide variety of adjustment problems. The range of possibilities is immense:

> Sally fails a math test, Sam forgets his review sheet again, Paul is tardy for the third time this week, Peter swears at his English teacher, George is upset because all his classmates "hate" him, Susan receives a "B" grade on a term paper and is in tears because she did so poorly, Henry receives a "D" on a quiz and announces that he is going to "party" next week because he is finally passing the course, Ricky is depressed because he cannot get into a Spanish IV course, Joe wants to quit school because sophomores can't take Auto Shop.

Whether or not these are adjustment problems for these students is hard to determine. But each time a student presents a problem to you, you must decide what to do about that problem: take action or ignore it. Now, if Sally attempts suicide, and Sam fails math for the second time, our roles as adults become a little more clear; these students need help! Likewise, if Paul is tardy 75 percent of the time, and Sarah misses 100 school days, you know something is wrong.

DECIDING WHAT CONSTITUTES
AN ADJUSTMENT PROBLEM

Anything you worry about may potentially be a problem. But it is important to find a balance between the extremes of worrying about every little developmental step and ignoring glaring signals that a student may be experiencing a serious adjustment problem.

> For example, practically every student is nervous on the first day of school: a normal developmental milestone. However, if the student frequently vomits at the sight of a school bus, that is not normal!

The following criteria will help you tell the difference between a normal behavior and one that might indicate that the student has an adjustment problem.

Criterion 1. Danger

Does the behavior appear to place the student or other students in danger? Will the problem have an immediate effect on the student's emotional health or physical welfare?

Criterion 2. Mobilization

Watching for the effect of students' behavior on the larger system of people around them is the primary tool for determining the severity of a symptom. What does this symptom cause other people to do? How many adults are mobilized into action? By determining the strength of the effect, you can gauge the potential severity of an adjustment problem. Realizing that a behavior is powerful, and therefore requires a response, is the initial step in mobilizing resources to help students. If a student consistently motivates you to pay attention and to discipline him, it may indicate that he has a weakness in his capacity to provide control from within. Furthermore, if he fights you for control, it may mean that his life is so out of control that professional help is needed.

Criterion 3. Persistence

The third way to determine the severity of a symptom is to notice whether or not it persists when you have taken some appropriate action to help the student. If the problem can be eliminated quickly and easily, even if the student has mobilized many adults, it is not as serious as one that seems to continue no matter what you do.

It is important to remember that what might sound like a serious problem may not be if we can treat it quickly and successfully. Conversely, some problems that appear insignificant can be serious if all attempts to treat them fail. Here is an example of a problem that seems quite serious but was treated quickly:

> Tom was sent down to the principal's office again. This was the third time in one week. He was sure to be suspended this time. The principal had warned him that if he continued to disrupt math class by laughing and blurting out comments to his friends, he would be sent home. His mother and father had also told him he would be grounded and lose all T.V. privileges if he didn't settle down in math. But he could not do this. He hated math. He just could not understand how to do the problems when the teacher explained them and wrote them on the board. He was angry and embarrassed and very uncomfortable sitting there. The only way to deal with his frustration and reach the end of the period was to "goof off." It was worth it, even if he lost T.V., and he knew his parents would stick to that punishment.

Tom seems to have a serious problem. Fortunately, because of the suggestion made by his teacher, one of the learning disability teachers was consulted. It was discovered that Tom had a difficult time understanding spoken directions. So, when the teacher explained the math concepts, Tom might as well have been in a third-year Greek course. He could not see the examples on the blackboard because he always sat in the back of the room where he thought he could fool around more. When he was moved to the front of the room and encouraged to copy his notes from those recorded by another student, his comprehension of math improved along with his grades and behavior. With minimum effort on the part of the teacher and a school specialist, Tom's problem ended.

This is an example of a school adjustment problem that appeared very serious but, with competent action by the teacher, ceased to be a problem. In this next case Bob appears to have an insignificant problem, which in time develops into a very serious one.

> Bob is a 12-year-old who brought a pen to math class instead of a pencil with eraser. Initially, everyone thought this was insignificant, and Bob was gently reminded to bring in the pencil. During this time Bob was experiencing great difficulty keeping his math problems organized on his paper because instead of erasing mistakes, he was crossing them out and starting certain steps over again on a different part of the paper. It was impossible for either Bob or his teacher to tell if he was following the prescribed steps for completing the problems because the paper was such a mess. He continued to do this even though he was disciplined by his teacher and scolded by his parents who were eventually notified of his problem. Bob was not acquiring a knowledge of either the thinking or written steps necessary to execute his math problems. He dropped farther and farther behind. In Bob's case his poor performance in math damaged his self-esteem as well as his grades. Even though the school began to assign detentions to Bob for not having the proper writing imple- ments in class and the parents disciplined him at home, he continued to have the problem.

Bob's bringing a pen to math class had serious implications because it was a behavior that persisted when attempts were made to change it.

Determining if a student has an adjustment problem is an ongoing process of continual assessment. Using the criteria of *potential danger* to the student, *resistance* to help, and *mobilization* of adults will help you with this difficult task. But it is difficult to assess a student's behavior unless it can be described in clear and specific terms.

DEFINING SPECIFIC BEHAVIORS

Developing specific descriptions of behavior is important for the following reasons:

The possibility of misinterpretation is reduced if you present specific and observable behavioral descriptions. John's being disrespectful can mean "he didn't stand when an adult entered the room" or it could mean "he made an obscene gesture to a passing motorist!"

Misinterpretation of general statements can cause you to focus on the wrong behavior. Observable behaviors do not require complicated psychological interpretations to describe a student's problem or to change a behavior. If you see and describe a behavior, "not standing," and want it changed, "stand next time," there can be little argument as to whether or not that happens. It is a moot point in many cases as to whether or not it represents something greater than it is, be it disrespect or the casual laid-back attitude of today's youth.

It is therefore important to practice defining specific behaviors so that a student's problem can be discussed with parents and staff members in a clear and concise way. Clear descriptions of behavior also make it possible to develop specific goals. With goals stated in terms of observable behaviors, it is possible to measure change or to determine if any improvements have been made. The following steps will help you to do this:

Make a General Statement About the Problem. Imagine yourself talking on the telephone to a good friend and just blowing off steam about the problem you are worrying about:

"Hi, Betsy, I just called to say how discouraged I am getting about Paul. No matter what I tell him to do, he doesn't seem to do it. It makes me so mad that he's so disrespectful to me. I can ask him a dozen times to".....

Write Your Description in General Terms. "Paul is disrespectful because he doesn't do what I say."

Describe the Problem in More Detail. Do this in the same way you might try to describe to your mechanic that "funny" sound you heard under your car. If you don't force yourself to be specific about the kind of noise and its location, both you and your mechanic will become very frustrated, and the car might not be repaired. Just as the phrase "funny noise" is not specific enough for the mechanic, the word "disrespectful" is not specific enough to define the student's behavior clearly. Start with the word "disrespectful" and give a detailed description of what the student did that you regard as disrespectful. For example, you might say, "I have a student in my room who ignores me when I ask him to be quiet. When I tell him to come to my desk, he makes an obscene gesture and stays in his seat!"

Test the Accuracy of Your Description. Ask yourself what the student would have to *stop* doing or *start* doing to *convince* you that the behavior was improving. Say "If _____ stopped doing _____, I would have to agree that, at least for the moment, things would look better! For example;

"If Paul would stop ignoring me in class, stop making obscene gestures, and come to my desk when I ask him to, we will have solved that problem!"

Additional Examples of Descriptions.

General Descriptions	Specific Descriptions
Uncooperative	Refuses to open textbook
Disrespectful	Tells principal to "bug off"
Lazy	Is unwilling to copy over paper
Aggressive	Pushes a student out of line
Distractible	Looks up from book when someone coughs
Hostile	Ridicules others for missing a question in class

There is nothing wrong with speaking in general categories when discussing a problem, but before you can really understand a behavior, some attempts must be made to intervene and change that behavior. A specific observable behavior must be identified before that can happen. The following is a drill that will give you practice at recognizing whether or not a statement is specific or general. Both the exercises and the explanations will prepare you to organize your observations of a student's problem behavior.

Place a piece of paper over this page and move it down until you come to a question. Attempt to do each problem without exposing the explanation. The mark ///////// will tell you that the explanation is presented on the next line. Once you have read the explanation of the right answer, go on to the next question.

Compare the two statements and select the more specific one.

1. Harold is preoccupied.

   Harold won't answer when spoken to.

   ///

   Explanation: Statement two is more specific because it describes the exact behavior Harold is exhibiting.

2. Barb is sharpening 50 pencils.

   Barb is avoiding starting her English assignments.

   ///

   Explanation: Sharpening pencils states specifically how Barb is avoiding her homework; statement one is more specific.

3. Al argued that he had already cleaned his locker.

   Al said removing his gym clothes was "cleaning out his locker."

   ///

   Explanation: The second statement tells us exactly how the student has convinced himself he has complied with the task he has been given. To him "cleaning out" represents only removing the gym clothes. With this argument he would hope to be excused from consequences for not complying. Statement 2 helps the adult to see specifically how the student has analyzed the task and where his reasoning falls short.

4. Sallie is unable to record directions presented verbally by her teacher although she has no problem when they are written on the board.

   Sallie has difficulty with aural discrimination in algebra class.

   //

   Explanation: While both statements are fairly specific, statement 1 leaves no question as to exactly how the listening problem affects the student. It also gives a specific task to focus on during treatment.

5. Pete looks up at any student who makes a noise or movement during study hall.

   Pete is impulsive and distractible and cannot complete assignments while in study hall.

   //

   Explanation: Statement 1 tells *how* Pete is impulsive and distractible.

6. Susan is depressed.

   Susan sits quietly in the back of the room, has a sad look on her face, and refuses to participate in any way.

   //

   Explanation: The specific behaviors that might constitute depression are outlined in statement 2.

7. Chris does not take notes or complete his worksheets in class.

Chris is lazy, uncooperative, uninvolved, and disrespectful and has a 48.5 average in math.

///

Explanation: While the second statement includes many adjectives, it does not specifically tell the reader what Chris does or does not do, as does statement 1.

After completing this exercise you should be able to make clear specific descriptions of worrisome behaviors. Narrowing down general concerns to specific observable behaviors is an important skill for management of students.

LOOKING FOR PROBLEM AREAS

The eight sketches of students with serious school adjustment problems in Chapter 1 present descriptions of behavior that make it fairly obvious that a problem exists. But you seldom start with completed summaries of a student's behavior. You start with isolated incidents of individual behaviors. It is difficult to know what each little incident means. In the same way a detective must gather little bits and pieces of information before he or she can understand the whole case, you must also start with small pieces. In the course of teaching you may have seen students do the following:

Not follow directions; blame other students for their mistakes; blurt out comments in class; overreact to distractions; cheat; refuse to complete tasks; become upset over small things; tease other students; fall asleep in school; claim other students are talking about them; make careless errors; speak unclearly; visit the school nurse too often; act sullen or unhappy; or react to criticism in an overly sensitive manner.

All these behaviors should raise a red flag when you scan for problem behaviors. But there are also hundreds of other behaviors that might mean a student has a problem. Some of them are insignificant, but others provide you with major clues as to what is troubling a student.

List of Symptoms Indicating Adjustment Problems

The following list of individual problem behaviors is organized into categories. As you scan the list you can note which specific behaviors characterize the student you are concerned about. It will help you to pinpoint specific behaviors and refer you to a next step according to how serious the behavior is. If you have identified a problem already, the list will help you to start to determine how serious it is.

There are 13 clusters of behaviors that represent a wide variety of problems students may experience. Scan the list and place a checkmark next to behaviors that concern a specific student. (The reader has permission to copy this list for their personal use in screening students for adjustment problems.)

General Category	Specific Descriptions
Uncooperative	+ **Does not follow directions**
	+ **Argues with directions**
	+ **Becomes angry when told what to do**
	+ **Hears what he or she wants to hear**
	+ **Denies hearing what teacher said**
	○ **Tells teacher the curriculum is poor**
	+ **Claims not to have proper materials**
	+ **Says teacher is not teaching properly**
	+ **Blames others for mistakes/ problems**
	○ **Tells adults they cannot boss him or her**
	+ **Tells teacher what to do**

General Category	Specific Descriptions
Impulsive	+ Does not sit still
	+ Blurts out/speaks out of turn
	+ Interrupts
	+ Gets out of seat without permission
	○ Works on assignments only for a few minutes
	+ Forgets things frequently
	+ Loses things frequently
	+ Looks around room often
	+ Always laughs when others clown
	○ Reacts to all distractions
	○ Is extremely excitable and lacks self-control in new situations
Poor peer relations	○ Tries to make other students laugh
	○ Gets others to tease or hit him or her
	+ Complains of being picked on
	○ Patronizes adults, but angers peers
	+ Interrupts other students' activities
	+ Cheats in games
	○ Is unwilling to agree on rules for games
	○ Cries too easily
	○ Exaggerates reports of how others treated him or her
	+ Claims all the kids hate him or her
	○ Constantly makes annoying and distracting sounds in class
	+ Coughs, burps, clears throat often
	○ Is avoided by other students
Hyperactive or attentional problems[1]	○ Is easily distracted
	○ Finds difficulty in completing tasks
	○ Appears not to understand directions
	○ Confuses details or sequence of steps

General Category	Specific Descriptions
	○ Cannot concentrate
	○ Cannot sit still
	○ Is loud and disruptive with other students
	○ Blurts out in class
	○ Is excitable and acts before thinking
	○ Cannot organize work
	○ Has difficulty waiting for his or her turn
Anxious	○ Fidgets or shakes often
	○ Expresses many unrealistic fears and worries
	+ Looks preoccupied
	○ Cannot tolerate frustrating situations
	○ Has difficulty telling the difference between important and unimportant things
	○ Reports "butterflies" in stomach often
	+ Is accident prone
	+ Becomes upset over small things
	+ Is overly concerned about details
	○ Cannot tolerate making mistakes
	○ Is overtired: reports not sleeping well
Antisocial	+ Teases other students
	○ Abuses others verbally
	− Threatens, bullies, and hurts others
	+ Makes obscene gestures
	− Lies, cheats, and steals
	○ Blames all problems on others
	○ Is cooperative when directly observed, but untrustworthy otherwise

General Category	Specific Descriptions
	+ Denies having any problems
	− Runs away for several days
	− Sets fires
	− Hurts animals
Withdrawn/depressed[2]	○ Cries easily and is easily hurt
	○ Avoids contact with adults and peers
	○ Reports being overtired or ill often
	○ Falls asleep in school
	− Absent often; tardy to school often
	+ Puts minimal effort into work
	+ Achieves below potential
	+ Reports illness to parents that is hard to document
	− Has chronic stomach or bronchial complaints
	○ Does not eat properly
Severe disturbance	− Says people are always talking about or watching him or her
	− Reports hearing voices
	− Imagines events that did not occur
	− Distorts events dramatically
	− Has very rapid shift in moods from happy to sad
	− Sits long periods of time without moving or speaking
	− Suddenly becomes violent
	− Speaks in a nonsensical language
	− Talks of suicide
	− Inflicts pain on self
	○ Is so preoccupied that he or she does not respond to being spoken to
	− Becomes extremely concerned and upset with minor details
	− Makes inappropriate sexual statements or overtures

General Category	Specific Descriptions
	− Is overly concerned about weight and experiences dramatic weight loss
	− Overeats, then vomits
	− Inflicts pain on others
Learning disabilities	+ Cannot follow directions
	○ Appears to have mastered a skill one day but cannot perform it the next
	+ Has poor handwriting or penmanship
	○ Does not line up math problem or write in straight lines on paper
	○ Reverses letters
	○ Does not raise hand to ask or answer questions
	○ Cannot repeat back to teacher simple directions
	○ Understands things that are spoken better than things that are written
	○ Understands things written better than things that are spoken
	+ Is impatient when being taught a new concept
	○ Can't seem to learn to tell time and/or is always late or confused
	○ Becomes lost or confused on playground
	○ Makes many careless errors
Language problems[3]	○ Does not use appropriate volume and pitch while speaking
	○ Speaks unclearly
	○ Cannot repeat short sentences correctly
	○ Does not follow directions
	○ Seems confused when given instructions

General Category	Specific Descriptions
	○ Cannot answer questions correctly or follow verbal instructions ○ Does not participate in class discussions ○ Struggles to find the word he or she wants to say ○ Cannot tell story in logical sequence ○ Seems embarrassed and disturbed by own speech ○ Has trouble rephrasing what others have said ○ Cannot order five verbal sentences in sequence ○ Has trouble telling the difference between cause and effect ○ Cannot explain meaning of a story or an event ○ Cannot tell basic facts about self: telephone number, address, parents' names, etc. (for students over age 7)
Physical problems	○ Squints and/or reports headaches ○ Reports dizziness often ○ Is very clumsy/accident prone ○ Has poor balance/frequently falls ○ Has poor manual dexterity ○ Is absent from school due to illness more than 10 percent of school days (approximately 20 days per year) ○ Visits school nurse more than two times per week ○ Is frequently excused from gym for medical reasons
Abused/neglected	○ Is often sullen or unhappy ○ Is overly sensitive to criticism

General Category	Specific Descriptions
	+ **Is unwilling to discuss personal affairs**
	+ **Defends parent when they are criticized**
	○ **Cannot tolerate making mistakes**
	○ **Reports bad dreams frequently**
	− **Is bruised**
	− **Loses self-control easily and goes into rages**

Note: each item on the list has a "+," "○," or a "−" code. These tell how serious a problem may be according to the following key:
+ = mild
○ = moderate
− = severe

[1]Adapted from the American Psychiatric Association, *Diagnostic and Statistical Manual of Mental Disorders,* 3rd ed. Revised (Washington, D.C.: APA, 1987)

[2]Joel Herskowitz, *Is Your Child Depressed?* (New York: Pharos Books, 1988). This is an excellent book on childhood depression, which is an underdiagnosed problem many school students face.

[3]Depending upon their age, all children may show some of these characteristics occasionally. A language, speech, and hearing specialist should be consulted if you notice the child doing many of these things consistently.

DECIDING HOW SERIOUS A PROBLEM IS

Now that you have located one or more problem behaviors, you are ready to decide what to do next. The codes next to each description refer you to the additional information to help you make that decision according to how severe the problem is.

"+" Codes: Mild Problems

The behaviors marked by the + code can either be considered typical for school-aged students or the first signs of a more serious adjustment problem. Whether or not they should be considered serious depends on the following considerations:

Age. A behavior that is normal for a fourth grader may be thought of as serious if an eighth grader consistently demonstrates it.

> When Harold is in fourth grade, it is more appropriate for him to cry when teased than it will be when he is in the eighth grade.

Consequences. A behavior that interferes with learning or disrupts the family is more serious than one that doesn't.

> If Pat forgets her homework regularly, but can make it up in study hall before class begins, the problem is minor. However, if she consistently earns bad grades, or her mother has to leave work to go home and bring the homework into school each time, that problem is more serious.

Duration. If a behavior presents a problem at school or at home, attempts should be made to change that behavior, even if you have decided that it is fairly typical or normal behavior. But, if it continues after you have taken reasonable steps to help the student, it should be considered more serious. The more a student resists attempts to help him or her change, the more reason for concern.

> Harry skips school to go fishing, is discovered, and is assigned a detention. If he serves the detention and stops skipping school, there is no real problem. If he continues skipping school, refuses to do the detention, and/or disobeys his parents when they try to discipline him, it is a reliable sign that an adjustment problem of major consequences may be starting to develop.

The behaviors that you have checked that are marked with a "+" need to be evaluated by you to determine how serious they are. Use the criteria of *age, consequences,* and *duration* to make your judgment.

Now you have the following choices: (1) Monitor the problem, but take no action to see if it eventually goes away by itself.

(2) Develop a program to help the student. (3) Refer the case to special education or to personnel from outside agencies. Whatever you do, keep the parents informed and invite them to participate on the team with school staff members you have gathered to help the student.

It is important to trust your natural instincts when making your decision. The student's behavior will eventually guide you toward the right plan of action whether or not you just monitor her or develop a treatment plan. You will know when things become better or get worse.

"○" Codes: Moderate Problems

These behaviors present a much higher probability that the student is under a significant amount of stress and is experiencing more difficulty in school than behaviors with the "+" codes. Therefore, it is important to investigate them further. Enlist assistance from the special services staff of your school. Request a meeting with the guidance counselor. Ask him or her to consult each other classroom teacher and the school principal to secure a progress report stating how the student is doing in all classes. Suggest that the guidance counselor invite any other teachers who have concerns about the student to join the meeting. Once again, it is crucial to enlist the participation of the parent for this case conference. (Chapter Seven will deal with engaging parents as members of your team.) The primary goal of the meeting is to work toward a description of the problem that is as specific as possible. Use the age, consequences, and duration criteria, as you did for mild problems, to evaluate the information you have gathered. Consult Chapter Three to begin to develop a plan to treat the student.

"—" Codes: Severe Problems

If you have checked behaviors with "−" codes, you have identified symptoms that probably characterize a student with serious adjustment problems. It should be emphasized that this does not necessarily mean the student is severely disturbed. But it does mean that a comprehensive team effort is necessary to understand and treat the problem. There should be coordination among the classroom teacher, parent, and any of the following school and community resource persons:

Guidance counselor or adjustment counselor

School psychologist

School principal and/or assistant principal

Family pediatrician

Community mental health or private therapist

District court probation department

Special education administration (Chapter Eleven presents discussion of support services available through special education)

The group you have formed with the guidance counselor should immediately seek further evaluation and diagnosis. Select one of the following options:

1. *If* the school can help, use its evaluation resources. This is usually a professional screening and assessment process through the department of pupil personnel services and/or department of special education.
2. *If* the school cannot help, the teacher should support the parent in an effort to obtain the name and address of the state's regional education office and/or a local student advocacy office.
3. *If* you and the parent are still worried after taking steps 1 and 2 and also believe the student's health and safety are in immediate jeopardy, encourage the parent to
   a. Contact a pediatrician *or*
   b. Contact the local division of social services *or*
   c. Call a children's emergency services hotline.
4. *If* you suspect that the child may be subjected to either abuse or neglect, contact your school administrator to discuss the possibility of filing an abuse and neglect petition with your local department of social services. The topic of child abuse and neglect is presented in Chapter 14.

If a service is recommended and parents are concerned about paying for this service, they should call their health insurance office and ask if their policy covers the service they require. But if the parents cannot pay and/or do not have health insurance coverage call this number, 1-202-628-8787, which will place them in contact with The Children's Defense Fund. This agency has updated lists of other agencies and resources in each state that provide students help on an emergency basis. Remember, you are one of the student's primary advocates. You should continue to seek help until you are satisfied that the helping agents are acting in "good faith" to assist the student. This does not mean that the problem will disappear suddenly. Some school adjustment problems can disappear quickly, but others require years of hard work on the part of the family and the school. Some never seem to get better.

Use the tools that Chapter One offers you to locate and define problems. Your ability to notice a problem someone else has overlooked can make a great difference for a student. By comparing a student's behavior to the behaviors listed on the problem behavior checklist, you can begin the process of finding help for the student. You can take your information to other concerned adults and begin to construct a team made up of the parent, school, and community.

Part II

TOOLS FOR CHANGE

3

Planning an
Intervention Program

This chapter will help you to become an active agent in changing the behavior of students. There are many styles of disciplining and working with students which are unique for each teacher. Consequently, it is impossible for anyone to be able to know what will work for any given classroom. That is why you will become the expert for the students you teach. But this means you will have to do most of the decision making and tailor an approach that is appropriate for your unique set of circumstances. This chapter will provide you with guidelines, so you can develop and evaluate your approach. There is a lot of "trial and error" involved in discovering what will work, and that is why it is important to remember that it is all right for procedures *not* to work out well at first. You will keep trying until you find a solution.

You can usually work out an effective approach as a classroom teacher or parent. The resources of your school's special services support personnel are also available. The remainder of the book deals with making use of these resources and building a team of adults to help students with problems that persist after you have tried to help.

As you read and apply the material of this chapter, keep these things in mind. As teacher, you are the final judge of what will work best in your situation. There are many guidelines and a variety of tools from which you can construct a plan of action to help a student with a problem. But ultimately, structure is the most important element of effective programs for students who are having problems.[1]

UNDERSTANDING STRUCTURE

Structure is defined as "a clear set of expectations and consequences to be used in response to a specific behavior." There are two kinds of structures: internal and external.

Internal Structure. This is the voice inside you that makes judgments about what to do and tips you off as to what will happen if you make the wrong decision; for example,

> "Gee, if I tell my friend Debbie that she has an ugly dress on, she will not want to go to the movies with me tonight!"

External Structure. This is the voice or rules of someone else that tells you what will happen if you make poor or irresponsible judgments about what to do; for example,

> "If you don't eat your peas, Tommy, there will be no dessert;" or "If you fail one more quiz, Gail, you won't pass math."

We live in a world of structures that surround and influence us constantly. Some of these are less clear than others. Being told by your boss that he expects hard work from all employees is a lot *less* specific than being told by a speed limit sign: "SPEED LIMIT 25." We, as adults, usually proceed with our daily routine with a general understanding of what rules mean. But there are times, when we really think about it, that we are not exactly sure what the boss means by "hard work" or even at what point the local police will decide that 25 miles per hour plus is too much above the limit. If we effectively interpret the rules and expectations that we live with on a daily basis, our lives go smoothly. But, if we make an error in judgment and take too much time at coffee break or drive to work at 34 miles per hour instead of 25, we might be reprimanded by an external source of structure, our boss or the local police.

This brings us to the first major idea about structure for students. Students do not always have the capacity to interpret unclear structures. They have not had the experience adults have had, which involves some trial and error. For example, you might get a speeding ticket if you interpret speeding as "more than 10 miles per hour over the speed limit" when the officer interprets it as "anything over 5 miles per hour over the limit." Similar experiences, during which we learn to interpret rules, provide most of us with a sense of how to avoid reprimands.

As students grow and develop a pool of information about what they can and cannot do, they also learn, to various degrees, how to work within the structures around them. However, some students have difficulty deciding how to behave because they cannot translate rules into guidelines for appropriate behavior. They may act in ways that are upsetting to themselves and to the adults around them, and therefore, alert parents or teachers to the possibility that they are under stress and in need of more external structure. It is a kind of human ecology where the student, in one part of a system, gives a message to another part of the system, the parents and teachers, to provide assistance.

The degree of structure students require depends on the amount of stress they are experiencing. The more they are stressed or afraid, the more structure their behavior will demand. As students begin to perceive that they are out of danger and experience less stress, their demand for structure reduces.

Sometimes *we* are surprised when a specific structure works for a student because they were convinced it would not work. There are many ways to develop specific consequences for students who are experiencing problems. It is best to adopt a trial and error approach to helping a student with a problem. In this way you can experiment with various ways of providing structure. Eventually your natural instinct and the student's persistence will guide you to a program that works.

SORTING SYMPTOMS

Before you try to change any behavior, it is important to decide which symptoms represent the most important problem to focus on. To decide which behavior to treat first, follow these steps:

1. List the behaviors you have identified when you scanned for problem areas.
2. Then choose a target behavior.
3. Write behaviors in clear terms and rank them starting with the most serious one first.

Here is an example of a list before and after sorting.

Sample List of Sorted Behaviors

UNRANKED	RANKED (most serious first)
Won't eat school lunches.	1. Uses skateboard recklessly.
Loses pencil and notebook.	2. Can't sleep at night.
Refuses to serve detention.	3. Daydreams in class.
Uses skateboard recklessly.	4. Won't serve detention.
Can't sleep at night.	5. Loses pencil and notebook.
Argues about rules.	6. Argues about rules.
Daydreams in class.	7. Won't eat school lunches.

Once the list of unranked behaviors is placed in order of severity, you can focus your efforts on the most important problem first. The most important behavior to control from the list is obvious: the reckless use of the skateboard. This may not be defined as a school or family adjustment problem, but it offers the greatest potential for bodily harm to the student. It also represents the student's lack of good judgment and incompetent management of his behavior.

As you may notice, some of the more serious symptoms on the list appear to cause the problem behaviors listed farther down. Students who can't sleep at night are more likely to daydream in school and to lose things because they are less attentive due to lack of sleep.

It may be tempting to focus on the problem behavior that annoys you the most. You may tend to focus on the student who constantly needs a pencil. There is no question that this behavior can be experienced by you as a problem deserving attention. Attempting to fix it can be exhausting and very time consuming. But if you allow the student to distract you totally with low-priority behaviors, it is difficult to focus on the more serious problems.

Once you have isolated a behavior and identified it as a high-priority problem, you are ready to construct a plan to help the student. A high-priority behavior will be referred to as a "target behavior" from now on.

Here is another exercise to help you sort out a high-priority behavior. Hal cannot complete his math problems at home. To determine whether or not this is the crucial aspect of his problem or merely a symptom of another problem, we have to gather more information and analyze it. All the following questions must be addressed before Hal's problem can be understood. After reviewing each question, rank them according to which behavior you think is the primary problem.

Does Hal sit down each night in a quiet place and attempt to complete homework?

Does Hal have the proper materials at home each night?

Does Hal still have his books, or has he lost them?

Does Hal hear and comprehend his assignments?

Does Hal understand the lessons presented in class?

Does Hal take notes in class and avoid talking with his friends during lectures?

Do Hal's notes reflect an understanding of what the math teacher is presenting?

Does Hal pass tests or quizzes and give his teacher any indication that he is learning?

Has Hal been asked to come for extra help, and has he been willing to do so?

Can Hal hear well enough to gain anything from the classroom presentations each day?

If you can say "no" to "Does Hal understand the lessons presented in class?" then you can see that the other questions are not relevant. Not doing math problems at home is really just the obvious symptom of another problem: Hal has no idea what is going on in math class in the first place. Helping the parent to set up a structure at home for Hal to complete math homework, such as no T.V. until homework is done, would surely fail because he cannot do the work. Teachers, with the help of parents, have to be active in the process of analyzing a student's problem. In Hal's case he never understood class presentations and never went for extra help. When you have sorted out what behavior represents a primary problem, it is time to develop a goal.

DESIGNING A PLAN FOR CHANGE

Developing Goals

The first step in developing a plan is for the parent or teacher to identify a goal for the student. The goal should relate to a specific and observable behavior (henceforth called a *target behavior*). The behavior must be clearly defined and one you can easily observe. It is imperative that you be able to tell if the student has made improvement and has accomplished the behavioral task you have asked her to do.

> Getting better grades is not as clearly defined as going to your English teacher twice a week for extra help on writing essays.

Your plan must also have goals that are realistic to attain. Request a small behavior change to be as sure as possible that the student can reach the goal. As each small step is made, add another. If the student fails too often, he will become discouraged and not invest as much effort in the program.

> Hal is not able to do his math problems at home because he doesn't pay attention in class. Instead of trying to reward him for completing all math homework, initially, he should be rewarded for attending extra help sessions after school several days a week.

Providing Regular Supervision

The plan should also provide for regular supervision of the student. The more often you (or some adult) can personally observe the behavior and judge whether or not the goal has been met, the more likely the student will respond to your effort to help him change.

> Telling Jack he cannot earn free time in tutorial unless he remains on task for 80 percent of the period will not work unless someone can observe him while he is working.

Providing for Consistency

The third aspect of an effective plan involves consistency of application. Develop a plan and stay with it so the student will know what to expect.

A written agreement between the student and the parent should be made. This agreement, called a *contract*, is designed to help avoid confusion about what you want the student to do. The next chapter is devoted to the use of contracts.

Note

1. Beth Sulzer-Azaroff and G. Roy Mayer, *Applying Behavior-Analysis Procedures with Children and Youth* (New York: Holt, Rinehart and Winston, 1977).

4

Using Contracts

Behavior contracts are written agreements between students and the adults working with them. They serve a number of purposes:

1. To provide an outline for a discussion between students and adults.

2. To identify specific behaviors necessary to help a student change behavior.

3. To provide a clear and succinct written record of agreed-upon details.

4. To encourage the student to take responsibility for his behavior.

5. To provide each party with a document outlining the details of the agreement for future reference.

Contracts help students to understand exactly what adults want them to do. Therefore, the process of developing a contract has application to almost any setting for any kind of behavior change.

SAMPLE CONTRACTS

The contracts provided here give you a representative sample of how contracts are used for a variety of different behavioral goals. You have permission either to copy or to adapt these samples providing they are used solely for individual students you work with.

Generic Contract

_____(name of student) hereby agree to the following behavioral contract.

Beginning on_____(date), I will do the following things:

  1.

  2.

  3.

  4.

I understand that it is completely my responsibility to do these things by_____(time) each week/day, and if I do, my parent/teacher will allow me to have the privilege of (list reward(s)):

This contract will be valid for a period of_____days. At that time the undersigned parties will renegotiate the conditions of this contract. It cannot be renegotiated earlier without the express agreement of all undersigned parties.

I have read and fully understand the conditions of this agreement.

SIGNATURES:

_____	_____
(student)	(date of signing)
_____	_____
(parent)	(teacher)
_____	_____
(parent)	(teacher)

SAMPLE CONTRACT 1: PARENT/CHILD CONTRACT FOR HOMEWORK COMPLETION

I, Al Duit, hereby agree to the following behavioral contract. Beginning on March 1, 1987, I will do the following things:

1. Complete my homework each night in math and English.

2. Secure signatures each Friday from my math and English teachers on my Weekly Monitoring Sheet documenting that my homework has been completed. (see Chapter 5 for sample monitoring sheets)

3. Deliver my monitoring sheet home each Friday and tack it to the bulletin boad in the kitchen.

   I understand that it is *my* responsibility to remind my teacher to sign my sheet and to deliver it home. I understand that if I forget it OR lose it, I will not get my reward EVEN if I have met all other conditions of my contract.

I understand that it is completely my responsibility to do these things by 6:00 P.M. on Friday night, and if I do, my parents will allow me to have the privilege of

going to the movies or a school-sponsored event with my friends on Friday night.

This contract will be valid for a period of 30 days. At that time the undersigned parties will renegotiate the conditions of this contract. It cannot be renegotiated earlier without the express agreement of all undersigned parties.

I have read and fully understand the conditions of this agreement.

SIGNATURES:

_____	_____
(Al Duit)	(date of signing)
_____	_____
(Mrs. Duit)	(Math Teacher)
_____	_____
(Mr. Duit)	(English Teacher)

SAMPLE CONTRACT 2: STUDENT/TEACHER FOR TALKING IN CLASS

I, Al Duit, hereby agree to the following behavioral contract. Beginning on March 1, 1987, I will

   1. Refrain from blurting out in remedial reading class. (This means I will reduce the number of times I speak out without raising my hand.)

I understand that it is completely my responsibility to do this during class each day; if I do, my teacher will allow me to have the privilege of

using the computer at the end of class to play games. The amount of time I earn will vary according to the following schedule:

No blurts	15 minutes
1 or 2 blurts	10 minutes
3 or 4 blurts	5 minutes
more than 5	no time

This contract will be valid for a period of 10 school days. At that time the undersigned parties will renegotiate the conditions of this contract. It cannot be renegotiated earlier without the express agreement of all undersigned parties.

I have read and fully understand the conditions of this agreement.

SIGNATURES:

_____   _____
(Al Duit)   (date of signing)

_____   _____
(Remedial Reading Teacher)

SAMPLE CONTRACT 3: PARENT/TEACHER/CHILD FOR APPROPRIATE BEHAVIOR IN SCHOOL

I, Al Duit, hereby agree to the following behavioral contract. Beginning on March 1, 1987, I will demonstrate appropriate physical self-control:

1. I will walk in the halls.

2. I will wait my turn by not pushing into lines.

3. I will not hit other students when I become angry.

4. I will take my monitoring sheet home each day. I understand that it is *my* responsibility to remind my teacher to sign my sheet and to deliver it home. I understand that if I forget it *or* lose it, I will not get my reward even if I have met all other conditions of my contract.

I also understand that it is completely my responsibility to do these things during school each day. If I do, my parents will allow me to have these privileges:

1. Watch my favorite T.V. show between 4 and 5 o'clock each afternoon.

2. Go roller skating on Saturday if I bring home a good monitoring sheet at least three days of the week.

A good monitoring sheet means that I did not do *any* of the things (run, push, or hit) that I am not allowed to do in school. This contract will be valid for a period of 14 days. At that time the undersigned parties will renegotiate the conditions of this contract. It cannot be renegotiated earlier without the express agreement of all undersigned parties.

I have read and fully understand the conditions of this agreement.

SIGNATURES:

_____   _____
        (Al Duit)   (date of signing)

_____   _____
      (Mrs. Duit)   (teacher)

SAMPLE CONTRACT 4: SPECIAL EDUCATION STAFF/STUDENT TO ENCOURAGE PARTICIPATION IN CLASS

I, Al Duit, hereby agree to the following behavioral contract. Beginning on March 1, 1987, I will do the following things:

1. Demonstrate to each of my special education instructors an effort to be "on task" 75 percent or more of each class period.

   I understand that to be "on task" I must make an effort to participate in classroom activities. These activities include:

   a. Listening when my teacher or other students speak.
   b. Attempting to complete written assignments.
   c. Answering questions when asked.
   d. Reading my book when told to do so.

I understand that it is completely my responsibility to do these things during each class day. If I do, my teacher will allow me to have the privilege of entering the recreation room for 15 minutes between each class.

2. I understand that if I am not able to demonstrate "on task" for at least 75 percent of the class time, then I will go to study hall instead of the recreation room. While in study hall, I agree either to sit quietly or to complete my homework assignments.

This contract will be valid for a period of five school days. At that time the undersigned parties will renegotiate the conditions of this contract. It cannot be renegotiated earlier without the express agreement of all undersigned parties.

I have read and fully understand the conditions of this agreement.

SIGNATURES:

_____   _____
        (Al Duit)   (date of signing)

_____   _____
        (parent)   (teacher # 1)

_____   _____
        (parent)   (teacher #2)

SAMPLE CONTRACT 5: THERAPEUTIC DAY STAFF/ STUDENT/PARENTS TO CONTROL VERBAL AND PHYSICAL ABUSE IN SCHOOL

I, Al Duit, hereby agree to the following behavioral contract. Beginning on Mach 1, 1987, I will do the following things:

1. Demonstrate appropriate social behavior in school.

If I become angry or upset with another student or a teacher, I will politely ask for a meeting to discuss the problem or request a "Time Out" so I can quietly sit alone and gain control of my behavior.

2. I will refrain from
    a. Swearing or making verbally inappropriate statements.
    b. Making obscene gestures.
    c. Pushing, striking, or physically intimidating other students.

3. I further understand that when I am not demonstrating appropriate social behavior the staff will assign me brief detentions (between 5 and 10 minutes per incident).

4. I agree to take home a monitoring sheet to let my parents know how many minutes in detention I receive each day. I understand that it is *my* responsibility to remind my teacher to sign my sheet and to deliver it home. I understand that if I forget *or* lose it, I will not get my reward *even* if I have met all other conditions of my contract.

I also understand that it is completely my responsibility to demonstrate appropriate social behavior all the time.

1. If I have less than 5 minutes in detention each day, I may use my skateboard after school.

2. If I have less than 10 minutes in detention each day, I may leave the house after school and play with my friends, but *may not* use my skateboard.

3. If I have between 10 and 30 minutes detention each day, I am campused to my house and cannot watch T.V. during the afternoon.

Continued

4. If I have more than 30 minutes in detention on any day, I must stay in my room after school until dinner and will lose my T.V. privileges for the evening.

This contract will be valid for a period of 14 days. At that time the undersigned parties will renegotiate the conditions of this contract. It cannot be renegotiated earlier without the express agreement of all undersigned parties. I have read and fully understand the conditions of this agreement.

SIGNATURES:

_____	_____
(Al Duit)	(date of signing)
_____	_____
(Mr. Duit)	(Special Teacher 1)
_____	_____
(Mrs. Duit)	(Special Teacher 2)

Behavioral contracts are useful tools that have a wide variety of applications. Like any well-written legal contract, they should contribute to a clear understanding of what various parties expect from one another. Value lies both in the process of discussing and negotiating the contract and in the behavioral structure it ultimately provides to the student. Contracts can be used for both young students and adolescents, for minor problems as well as major behavioral problems. The samples just presented are prototypes of contracts for different kinds of problems for students in various settings. They should be thought of as starting points for the development of your own contracts. An infinite number of variations are possible. Any time you need to make a clear and concrete agreement with a student, a contract can be employed.

PLUGGING THE LOOPHOLES STUDENTS FIND IN CONTRACTS

There are many times when you say the following:

> "I shouldn't have to do this; the student should be able to do this on his or her own."

> "I really don't think it's necessary to write this down on paper in the form of a contract. We have it clear in our heads."

> "Let's not get too picky. This is specific enough, and Bobby knows what I mean."

These are common reactions to the task of writing down the terms of a behavioral contract. However, it is recommended that the behavioral structures you develop with students be written down. Just the process of deciding what to put down on paper will force you to confront the many potential ambiguities that arise in negotiating any kind of contract. But, no matter how specific and clearly written, your contract with your student will have loopholes that he or she will exploit. This will put you into a bind·

> But, Mr. Jones, you said I had to have my homework finished by the day it was due. You didn't say I couldn't turn it in at the end of the school day after my class had met! After all, I did get it done."

While the student may have a "technical" point, she quite clearly did not follow the spirit of the agreement. This is a time when you have to decide whether or not "fairness" outweighs letting the student avoid responsibility.

At a time like this you have two choices. First, you will either attempt to be fair and back down from the consequences, or, second, you will stick to the agreement because you know that, even though there is a loophole, the student basically knew what was expected and is just taking advantage of the situation. Depending upon what you decide, these will be the results:

> If you back down, the student will give you plenty of opportunities to restructure her behavior because she probably will not make the behavior changes you want.

> If you do not back down, you may feel guilty for being "unfair" and acting like a cruel dictator. But if your structure is maintained, the student probably will make behavior changes, and you will know that you have helped.

Most of us need to experiment with both methods of resolving the conflict of the "loophole." Through trial and error you can determine how specific your particular approach needs to be. Students who continue to need your help find ways of getting that message to you, and, providing you are vigilant, you will know when to provide that help.

In summary, an effective program provides both you and the student with a clear, concise agreement. It charges each party with a realistic task. Either you or the parent can define exactly what you want the student to do. But choose a behavior that you can consistently observe and easily reinforce. Students are asked to perform a task that they can realistically accomplish, one they know they can do if they make a reasonable effort. They are then carefully observed and rewarded when they achieve the specified behavioral goal. Both parties have a written record of their agreement in the form of a contract. The process of preparing the contract provides both the student and the adult with a forum for identifying and discussing any ambiguities in the agreement. A well-constructed plan provides adults with a powerful tool for helping students with adjustment problems.

5

Using Rewards and Restrictions and Monitoring Behaviors

Behavioral contracts are useful tools only to the extent that they are supported by an appropriate use of disciplinary structures. Students with adjustment problems find it difficult to change their behavior without some use of external structure. It is common sense that if they could use internal controls successfully, they probably would not have surfaced in your classrooms as students with problems. Before we can help students who have adjustment problems, we need to acquire a better understanding of the use of rewards and restrictions.

REWARDS

Rewards are defined as privileges, presents, or activities to motivate the student to change his or her behavior. While many things can be thought of as "rewarding," as used here the term "reward" represents the payoff used in response to the student's performance on a specific task. Rewards must be as "pure" as possible and not confused with activities that have educational merit, nor should they restrict students from valuable family time. It is important for school staff to help parents learn to tell the difference. A pure reward, therefore, provides students with a payoff that is highly motivating but has little other value than to reward them for their behavior.

> If a student completes all math problems on time and accurately, the teacher might offer a "pure reward" of some free play time before the end of the classroom session. This kind of a reward or reinforcement is just for fun. Using a field trip or granting computer time to drill math problems is not a pure reward because there is intrinsic educational value to these activities. If the student were not to earn this type of reward, he would lose an educational opportunity.

At home, rewards like extra allowance or extra T.V. time might be considered as "pure rewards," but watching the evening news with the family would not. You do not want to allow a parent to jeopardize valuable family time by using it as a reward. Otherwise, the student and the family lose something of value if the "reward" is not earned. Selecting appropriate reinforcers by using pure rewards increases the strength of a behavior management plan.

RESTRICTIONS

Restrictions are disciplinary consequences that are designed to discourage negative behaviors or to motivate students to perform in positive ways if they have been unable to do so in the past. When choosing disciplinary consequences, keep the following in mind:

- Define the behavior you want to change.
- Think of several possible restrictions.
- Ask yourself, "Which of these possibilities would affect the student the most, but detract the least amount from a family or educational activity?"
- Avoid using school work as restrictions, for instance,

making the student write two pages about why he or she misbehaved places a negative meaning on writing.

Pure Rewards and Restrictions	Activities with Family or Those with Educational Value
Access to games/special toys	Playing games with family
Additional T.V. time	Watching T.V. with the family
Snacks	Helping with family jobs
Stickers/small gifts	Helping teacher after school
Extended bedtime	Field trips
Extended curfew	Extra homework
Extended phone privileges	
Additional allowances	

To keep rewards and restrictions "pure," avoid these pitfalls:

If a reward has educational or family value, it is difficult to withhold it continually from a student who has been unsuccessful in meeting the criteria to earn it.

If a restriction or "punishment" has any potential to reward a student, then the disciplinary structure set up to help the student may backfire. If, for example, a student is disruptive but also lonely and in need of attention, requiring him to come in after school may not be effective. Both parents and teachers need to be sensitive to a situation where the student is in need of more nurturing and attention; however, offering a punishment that functions like a reward will not help the student either.

In summary, selecting appropriate rewards and restrictions may be more difficult than it initially appears. Trying to find reinforcers that are "pure" requires careful thought. In some cases you must experiment to see if the rewards and restrictions you have developed are appropriate. An otherwise well-conceived plan to change behavior will fail if a student is deriving a reward from a restriction that the adult believes is a negative consequence.

Most discussions about how to discipline students raise questions for parents and teachers. The next section identifies some common questions, answers them, and provides a rationale for the answers.

QUESTIONS FREQUENTLY ASKED ABOUT REWARDS
AND RESTRICTIONS

Question 1: Isn't there something wrong when you have to bribe students to get them to do what you want them to do?

Yes, there may be something wrong, but not necessarily. Students may have a serious problem if you find it necessary to reward and punish them constantly for everything you want them to do. But all students require the guidance and structure of adults and do not necessarily have a serious problem because of this. As they grow and develop, they develop internal structures and become less dependent on adults. To offer rewards is not "bribing." The intention of a bribe is to influence people to do something that may go against their better judgment and may be immoral and/or illegal. The intention of a reward is to increase the possibility that someone will perform in a more competent and responsible manner.

Question 2: Won't students become dependent on a system of rewards and punishments and never learn to control their behaviors independently?

This is a possibility, but an unlikely one for healthy students who are growing and developing normally as a result of the combined influences of good parenting and teaching. The reward structures you set up for healthy students serve their purpose and eventually fade away naturally and gradually. Students with adjustment problems do become dependent on powerful external structures and must be carefully weaned over an extended period of time. There are only a few students who never function without constant supervision and structure.

Question 3: Won't it be damaging to my relationship with the student if I always play the role of policeman, judge, and jury?

That depends upon how you play that role and how often you must play it. If what you do works, and the student becomes more responsible, competent, and successful as a result, it will help your relationship. Even if the student is furious with you for applying the structure or disciplining her, you may be building a better relationship. Students need to know that they can trust you to be firm and consistent in your efforts to help them with their behaviors at times when they are having difficulty controlling themselves. If things never get better and you and the student are always angry with each other, then you must take other steps to deal with the problem.

Question 4: I have a student who does not understand why I discipline her. She says I am unfair. Should I still discipline her when she misunderstands my intentions?

Adults and students frequently see the same events differently. If adults disciplined students only at those times when students agreed to it, then adults would not be needed—students could take care of themselves. It is also unfair to the student for adults to perpetuate the illusion that all interactions in the world will appear to be "fair." Students continue to require adult supervision even during times when they think it is unfair. It would be much more unfair to allow the student to continue to fail when you might have helped her by being firm with your disciplinary structure.

MONITORING STUDENT BEHAVIOR

While it is important to understand how the use of rewards and restrictions can help students, it is impossible to carry out behavioral programs without a consistent flow of regular information about their performance. As you begin to develop plans to engage parents and position them as important members of your team, the use of monitoring sheets becomes vital. Before parents can be expected to carry out a behavior management program in their homes, they must have information concerning their child's performance.

This information also can be used to develop a diagnostic picture prior to beginning a management program or to serve as a source of follow-up information once a student has stopped a treatment program. When combined with the use of a behavior contract, the monitoring sheet supplies either parent or teacher with a critical source of information which is needed to carry out the conditions of a contract.

There are times when it is unnecessary, unrealistic, or impossible for you and parents to speak with one another on a daily or weekly basis. If students can be motivated to carry their own monitoring sheets, they can provide an informational link. Most students over the age of 10 can take the responsibility of delivering a monitoring sheet to their teachers and then back home again to their parents. Their success depends, however, upon a number of factors:

Motivation: The student's management program must offer a reward powerful enough to motivate the student to have his sheet signed and brought home.

Realistic Goals: The student must have a good chance of achieving the behaviors that are specified in the contract.

Consistency: Parents and teachers must carry out the conditions of the contract consistently. If the student believes she can talk the adults into getting a reward when she has forgotten or lost the sheet, the program will be undermined.

Responsibility: The student needs to bear the responsibility of reminding the teacher to sign the contract and of delivering it home. If the first three conditions are met, the student can be successful. How many times do students lose their money on the way to the corner store for an afternoon snack? One time usually cures the carelessness.

Monitoring sheets are valuable tools for adults and students. They give the student an important role in the behavior management program and provide regular information that is difficult for adults to retrieve otherwise. If they do not work, it is usually not due to the student's inability to carry the sheet home. It is more likely a result of the student's not being successful in school and/ or an ill-conceived behavior management program. Following are some sample monitoring sheets to use with parents.

SAMPLE MONITORING SHEET 1: Parent Weekly Monitoring of Student in a Single Subject (to be carried by student)

TO MY TEACHER:

Subject:

PLEASE CHECK ONLY IF I

_____ have completed and turned in my classroom work and homework on time.

_____ am actively participating in classroom activities.

_____ am maintaining at least a _____% average on tests quizzes and homework.

Thank you very much.

_____
Signature of Student

_____   _____
Signature of Teacher   Date

Comments:

SAMPLE MONITORING SHEET 2: Parent Weekly Monitoring of Student in Several Subjects (to be carried by student)

_____: Weekly Monitoring Sheet
(Student Name)

Date: Class 1 _____
Teacher Initials: _____

PLEASE CHECK IF

_____ my homework and classwork have been on time
        and prepared adequately.

_____ I have actively participated in classroom activities.

_____ I have maintained at least a(n) _____% average.

- -

Date: Class 2 _____
Teacher Initials: _____

PLEASE CHECK IF

_____ my homework and classwork have been on time
        and prepared adequately.

_____ I have actively participated in classroom activities.

_____ I have maintained at least a(n) _____% average.

- -

Date: Class 3 _____
Teacher Initials: _____

PLEASE CHECK IF

_____ my homework and classwork have been on time
        and prepared adequately.

_____ I have actively participated in classroom activities.

_____ I have maintained at least a(n) _____% average.

SAMPLE MONITORING SHEET 3: Parent Daily Sheet for Classroom Preparedness (to be carried by student)

To my teacher:

Please sign this monitoring sheet if I show you I have brought the following items to class each day:

1. A pencil and pen

2. My books

3. An assignment notebook

_____

(Signature of Teacher)

Thank you.

_____

(Signature of Student)

Comments:

SAMPLE MONITORING SHEET 4: Parent Daily Monitoring of School Behavior (to be carried by student)

_____   _____
(Name of Student)   (Date)

To: _____
Name of Staff Member

Please indicate below how many times I needed warnings for disruptive behavior today (examples: blurting out comments, throwing things around the room, making faces at other students, etc.).

_____
(Number of Times)

_____
Signature of Staff Member

Comments:

SAMPLE MONITORING SHEET 5: Special Teacher Monitoring Regular Class Behavior (to be passed between staff members)

MONITORING OF STUDENTS MAINSTREAMED INTO REGULAR CLASSES

STUDENT:_____

WEEK ENDING:_____

CLASS:_____

TEACHER:_____

ON TASK: PLEASE ESTIMATE THE PERCENTAGE OF TIME THE STUDENT STAYED ON ASSIGNED TASK DURING YOUR CLASS PERIOD. IF ABSENT WRITE "AB."

MONDAY:_____

TUESDAY:_____

WEDNESDAY:_____

THURSDAY:_____

FRIDAY:_____

ACHIEVEMENT: BASED ON PERFORMANCE ON TESTS, HOMEWORK, OR CLASSROOM ASSIGNMENTS, ESTIMATE A GRADE THIS STUDENT HAS EARNED FOR THIS WEEK.

A   90–100
B   80–90
C   70–80
D   60–70
E   BELOW 60

ADDITIONAL COMMENTS: IF YOU HAVE ANY ADDITIONAL COMMENTS OR CONCERNS, PLEASE ADD THEM OR CALL US AT _____

(Phone # of Special Staff)

These monitoring sheets may be used for different purposes. Each one has been tested extensively with students and staff and has proven to be an effective means of passing information on a regular basis.

You are encouraged to use any of the five sheets listed or to modify them to meet the needs of the student(s) with whom you work. Each sheet requires only a few minutes to fill out. Monitoring sheets need to be kept brief and simple. They are a valuable tool in any management program, but should not be the only way adults communicate. While they provide a regular flow of critical information and serve as a device to quickly identify problems, they do not replace the ongoing communication that must occur between team members.

6

Using the Tools for Change

Deciding what behavior management plan to institute is the final step in building a program for the student. It is the time when you combine what you know about identifying behaviors, writing contracts, choosing rewards, and selecting target behaviors. The following steps list each stage of developing a plan. Simple and direct methods of dealing with the student are listed first.

STEP 1. TALK TO THE STUDENT

Find a quiet place where you and the student can be alone. Sit down and tell her that you want to discuss how she has been doing in school.

STEP 2. EXPLAIN YOUR RECENT OBSERVATIONS

Explain that you have noticed that she has been having a difficult time doing something, (the target behavior). Explain why you want to help her. This is important because it helps the student to understand both the intentions and values of the adult. Students sometimes deny that they have a problem, and they may be surprised when you try to intervene to help them. They need to hear the way you describe your reasons for wanting to help.

> "Sally, in this science class we believe it is important to follow all safety procedures. In this way we can reduce the chances of an accident and maintain an orderly laboratory procedure. So please do not begin *any* experiment until I have finished explaining the directions and then tell you to begin!"

STEP 3. DEVELOP A PROGRAM TO HELP THE STUDENT

You have several options: (1) a structure without a reward, (2) a structure with a reward, (3) a structure with a negative consequence.

Structures Without Rewards

A structure without a reward involves telling the student what behavior must be changed, but not stating any reward or negative consequence for failing to make the change. Tell the student *specifically* what has to be changed. Describe the behavior you want this student to be able to show you to indicate the change has been made. Say how long she has to make the changes.

> Too general: "Sally, don't you think it might be a good idea to return those books?" More specific: "Sally, we want all fifteen of those overdue library books back by Friday after school."

Sally may or may not know what you meant by the first statement labeled "too general." If there is any potential for students to misinterpret something a parent or teacher has asked them to do, they will more than likely do so. The general statement leaves the following potential loopholes or ways students can choose to interpret the command in such a manner as to believe they don't have to act on it:

Sally might not "think" it's a good idea to get the books back right away because she may believe the librarians don't really care since they have so many other books.

She might take some of the books back, but not all fifteen that are overdue.

Sally may be "intending" to take the books back, but just not quite as soon as her teacher might be expecting.

Sally might find many other ways to ignore her teacher's request to return the books if she really doesn't want to take them back.

Of course, there are times when students know what the adult means and consequently act on a nonspecific command. But these are not the kinds of situations that cause conflicts. It is the times when you believe you have stated instructions clearly, and students do not follow them that cause problems. You may have inadvertently left many loopholes in the mind of the student as to exactly what you want done. If directions are not being followed, state them in precise detail with specific times indicating when they must be carried out. If that doesn't work, go to the next option.

Structures With Rewards

Provide a structure with a reward. Tell the student specifically what has to be changed. Describe the behavior you want this student to be able to show you to indicate the change has been made. Say how long he has to make the changes. Specify the reward to be provided if the behavioral goal is accomplished. Write down the conditions of the agreement in the form of a written contract.

"If you can complete all 50 math drill problems at 80 percent accuracy on the computer, you may play a game for 10 minutes."

A reward adds more power to the behavioral structure you have designed for the student. It would be great if students would always comply with your wishes when given a simple verbal request. However, there are times when they are not able to mobilize their internal resources well enough to organize and motivate themselves to carry out their assigned tasks. An external reward can add additional motivation to help the student begin a task. There are times, however, when the students cannot function even with the added bonus of a reward system.

STRUCTURES WITH NEGATIVE CONSEQUENCES

Provide a structure with a negative consequence. Tell the student *specifically* what has to be changed. Describe the behavior you want this student to be able to show you to indicate the change has been made. Say how long he has to make the change. Outline exactly what privilege will be lost if the goal has not been reached in an agreed upon period of time. Write down the conditions of the agreement in the form of a contract.

> "Students who do not have their first drafts completed and turned into me by next Friday will lose the privilege of going to the library for a free period next week."

Negative consequences are used if positive rewards are either not available or ineffective. By stating a negative consequence, you emphasize to students the importance of changing their behavior. Going to the trouble of arranging a behavioral contract that has clearly outlined consequences lets students know how committed you are to helping them become successful. Students who initially may be angry because you are trying to "force" them to do something may be relieved once they begin to be successful by starting to make positive behavioral changes. If you have provided a carefully thought out behavioral structure with appropriate negative consequences and the behavior does not change, then you are beginning to uncover the possibility of a more serious adjustment problem. Add multiple negative consequences as outlined in the next option.

Multiple Negative Consequences Repeat the steps you have just taken but add a second negative consequence. If things still do not improve, add additional consequences. Use the following guidelines for this:

Have you given the previous steps enough time? In many

cases students will "test" you to see how consistent you will be with their structures. You have to find a balance between stopping the treatment too quickly and letting things go too long. If the student neglects to meet the behavioral goal three or four times in a row, strengthen your set of consequences.

Have you used restrictions that you judge to be both appropriate for the student and realistic for you to carry out?

STEP 4 EVALUATE YOUR RESULTS

Through a systematic trial and error approach you have attempted to help the student. Initially you identified a behavior and asked the student to change it. Next you added rewards; then negative behavioral consequences. You have generated valuable information about what the student will or will not do in response to your effort. If students have demonstrated that they have met the goal you set up for them, go to step 5, removing structure. If the treatment is not going well, you may be dealing with a serious problem. This is discussed in step 6.

STEP 5 REMOVE THE STRUCTURE YOU HAVE CREATED

Removing the structure is just as important as creating it. Many positive gains are lost because we reduce our efforts to maintain structure and/or remove it too quickly. Evaluate the following possibilities to determine how to phase the student out of a behavior management program.

If the student appears to be happy and productive with the results of your classroom disciplinary structure, continue your program for a while. Many students feel safer and happier when you have expectations for them that help them behave in a competent way. That does not mean they will not complain sometimes and even beg you to change the structure. If the structure is not a burden on you and the student *looks* good, regardless of how much he complains, continue with the structure.

If it is difficult or a burden to keep the disciplinary structure *and* things have improved, it's time to *gradually* remove the structure. Follow these steps:

1. Tell the student that you feel she is doing much better.

2. Then observe her behavior for the next several days. If she feels secure about her behavioral changes, these changes will endure. If she believes that she cannot maintain positive change, just being told that she is doing better may cause the old behavior to return. In this case, you should continue your program because the student has not developed enough internal control to maintain the behavior without your structure.

3. If her behavior changes endure, tell her you are going to see if she is responsible enough to manage her behavior without the behavioral structure for a limited amount of time.

4. If you have no problems after a trial period of no structure, you can continue to remove the structure gradually. If problems reappear, remember you have previously been successful in treating this behavior and you can be successful again.

TROUBLESHOOTING FOR SERIOUS PROBLEMS

Severe problems are defined as problems that either do not respond to treatment and/or place students in physical or psychological danger. Therefore, it is sometimes necessary to use a trial and error approach to evaluate the severity of a problem. Teachers, usually with the help of the guidance counselor, need to find and try new approaches even when problems and setbacks are experienced. If you have consistently applied a program to help students change and they continue to experience a problem, then it is necessary to get more help. Use the following checklist of questions to help you evaluate the approaches you have previously used.

1. Are you sure the behavior you are trying to change has been defined clearly?

2. Have you written down in your contract exactly what you have asked the student to do?

3. Are you sure he understands what is expected?

4. Have you arranged a disciplinary consequence that you have been able to supervise and consistently carry out?

5. Have you been able to resist backing down when the student argues or begs you to give him a second chance?

If you have answered "no" to any of the five questions, you may have found an explanation as to why your present program is not working. You may have a good behavioral plan, but need to tighten up the way you execute it. But there are times when the student requires intervention beyond what you can easily do as teachers, even with the support of parents. It is important to have a method for determining when to seek additional help and to abandon the plan on which you are working. If, after a reasonable amount of time, the student does not improve and any of the following questions can be answered "yes," a referral for additional help may be necessary.

1. Has the student's problem become more serious since you began your program?

2. Has the student developed any new problem areas?

3. Has the problem started to have a significant negative effect on the student's classmates, family members, or playmates?

4. Do you feel, in your role as the teacher or counselor, that you have too much to handle and not enough energy to handle it?

If you have answered "yes" to any of these four questions, you may need to consult your school's department of pupil personnel services.

Throughout the process of looking for and deciding what to do about problems, you have uncovered many possibilities. However, some adjustment problems are persistent enough or serious enough that adults need to work together in teams. Chapters Seven through Nine each discuss the use of collaborative teams and support services. Initially, you will be encouraged join forces with the student's parents. If you encounter persistent or serious problems, Chapter Ten will guide you through the process of working with your department of pupil personnel services. Chapter Eleven presents an extension of this process for students who qualify for special education services.

Once students with adjustment problems have been identified and have not responded to your efforts to treat them, it is crucial to find some way to enlist the support of the parent. Doing this, however, is frequently an extremely difficult task. Chapter 7 addresses this problem.

Part III

TEAMWORK

7

Engaging the Parent

There have been four times this month that Jane has received a call from the school about Tom, her son in the seventh grade. Now every time the telephone rings, she is overcome by a sense of dread, fearing that it is someone from school calling. She wonders how much more a parent can do. She points out to her friends that the members of the school staff have always been able to reach her when there was a need. Twice she left her job with only 10 minutes notice to attend an emergency conference with the principal. She attended all four of the meetings with the school's special services staff and even tried to follow their advice on how to make Tom do his homework. There is a limit to her time, energy, and patience.

Initially, she believed everything the school said about Tom, but now she has her doubts. It is not as if she were one of those angry, argumentative parents who spend hours and hours trying to find some way to attack public educators. She has worked with the school faithfully for several years now. But Tom seems worse than before.

Jane not only feels upset that Tom is having problems, but also is beginning to doubt herself. She wonders if she has done something wrong to her son. Why does she feel guilty, embarrassed, and to blame for everything that goes wrong at school? After all she has no problems with Tom at home. He is friendly and polite and does not get into trouble in the neighborhood.

Jane does not know it yet, but she is quickly sliding into the role of a "resistant parent," one who will not do what the school people want her to do and who blames the school for Tom's problems. And why shouldn't she be resistant? She has done everything within her ability, and Tom continues to have serious school adjustment problems. Any of us who has faithfully worked to solve a problem of any kind and has continually failed would feel as Jane does. It is natural to become discouraged and angry.

The telephone rings. Jane rolls her eyes and wonders if this call concerns school. It does. Her heart sinks. She feels as if a ton of bricks has just landed on her. It is Mr. Donohue, the assistant principal. He explains that Tom has been sent down to his office once again. It seems that Tom couldn't stop making funny faces during his math test. Mr. Donohue asks Jane if she is sure she has been cooperating with Tom's special services teacher. He clearly implies that otherwise Tom would not be misbehaving and that Jane should really become a little more involved and cooperative.

Well, if that doesn't burn Jane! Boy, would she like to give Donohue a piece of her mind! How could he be in his right mind and even question her degree of cooperation. To hell with following every whim and fancy of those school people! What do they know anyway? If they did their jobs properly, Tom would be receiving better grades, and she would not be harassed so often.

A few minutes before the phone call Mr. Donohue sits in his office wondering how to deal with Tom's situation. He is frustrated and does not know how to approach this problem. As his mind wanders, he concludes that he generally likes his job as assistant principal, with the exception of times like this. He hates calling parents who think they are cooperating with the school but really are not. He wonders how to be friendly and supportive but at the same time put a little heat under folks to motivate them to work more productively with the school staff. He knows that Jane believes she has done everything she can do. She comes into school and meets with the staff when there is a crisis, and she maintains an interested and respectful attitude.

What could he say to her! Tom has acted up once again in math class. His teacher could not control his silliness and disruptiveness during a math test. He understands that it is really not Tom's fault. His learning and emotional problems make it next to impossible for him to do well in math. Taking tests is extremely difficult for Tom and always makes him feel stupid. So he does the only thing he knows to cope with this painful experience—he becomes goofy and avoids the test. In a way both Mr. Donohue and Tom are in a bind. Tom cannot handle taking tests, but he is required to do so. Mr. Donohue has no ideas about how to approach Jane, but he is required to call her to report the incident.

He wishes he could find some way to motivate this mother to follow the school's recommendations. They have been trying to persuade her to grant permission for an extensive educational assessment, but she keeps "forgetting" to send in the consent papers. In addition, she claims she cannot visit the school adjustment counselor once a week due to her busy schedule. Unless she does these things he feels there is very little hope for Tom.

Mr. Donohue finally decides to suggest subtly to Jane that she might cooperate a little more. But he really has no idea how to go about this task. He has had no training for this part of his job and wishes he could simply avoid the issue. He is annoyed that Tom and Jane have put him in this position and wonders why parents just don't do what the school staff wants them to do in the first place. Students would be happier, and he would not have to agonize over how to find an inoffensive way to tell people like Jane what to do.

DEALING WITH DIFFERENT POINTS OF VIEW

This story can be told by parents or teachers in one form or another throughout school systems all over the country. However, there are many problems that cannot be dealt with effectively unless the parent is drawn into the team of adults who are trying to help the student.

To break the impasse that Jane and Mr. Donohue face is very difficult. Many teachers who feel that they have a fairly good sense of how to help a student cannot do so when the parent attacks them and blames them for the student's failures. It is difficult to know how to develop and implement a plan of action when you find yourself trapped in a battle of wills with the parent. Once a cycle is established in which the parent and the teacher are angry with one another, efforts to help the student become crippled.

A parent sees the educational process from a different point of view than does the classroom teacher. Teachers have a constant source of firsthand information about the student as they teach that student each day. But teachers also must balance the needs of the individual with those of the entire class. Parents, on the other hand, depend upon their child's perception of school events for most of their information. It is also the parents' role to be an advocate for their own child, not for the class of students as a whole. It is reasonable to assume that, even in the best of working relationships, parents and teachers will sometimes experience conflicts when working with one another. The story of Jane and Mr. Donohue illustrates how problems can grow over a long period of time. Jane believes she is cooperating with the school, and Mr. Donohue believes he is doing the right thing by putting a little more pressure on her. As they struggle to help Tom with his adjustment problem, each party becomes more and more frustrated. Once they begin to polarize and become angry with one another, the chances of helping Tom are reduced.

Unfortunately, problems can occur much faster than they did for Jane and Mr. Donohue. In the next case, trouble starts as soon as the parent walks into the school building.

> After Mr. Brown received his daughter Barbara's report card, he decided that he would take the initiative to call her sixth grade teacher. The report said that Barbara "was not working up to expectations in math." When he reached the teacher, he said he wanted to discuss his daughter's math situation. Several days later on his way into the conference, he bumped into the school adjustment counselor, who informed him that he would also be attending the meeting. The counselor explained that the teacher requested his presence to support Mr. Brown, who clearly gave the impression that he was agitated about the school's math program. Mr. Brown had no questions about the math program and only wanted to find out how he could help Barbara do better. When he first

entered the school building, he was very calm. When he discovered that the school believed that he was about to confront them, he became agitated. Feeling defensive as he tried to clear up this misunderstanding, he convinced the school staff that he was, indeed, an "agitated parent coming to discuss the school's math program."

As the adjustment counselor noticed how much Mr. Brown struggled to explain himself, he was able to realize that maybe they had misunderstood his intentions. He told Mr. Brown that they had just had a very difficult meeting about their math program with an angry parent last week and were a little wary. He mentioned that they may have prematurely concluded that Mr. Brown was angry and could now see that he was merely concerned about his daughter's math and not there to attack the entire program. Mr. Brown relaxed and they had a productive parent conference.

This is a case where both the school staff and the parent are well intentioned. But a conflict situation still arose. Fortunately, the adjustment counselor recognized the misunderstanding and corrected it.

As we all know, there are many other cases where the parent is not as cooperative as Mr. Brown. Some parents come into the school for their initial meeting feeling angry. Others do not even want to talk to school staff. It is hard to know what to expect. We know that there will always be a group of students whom we simply cannot reach no matter what we do. But within each school population, there is a group of students with adjustment problems who may be difficult to help, but can be helped, especially if their parents can be engaged as part of a team of teachers and support staff. The more severe a student's school adjustment problem, the more important it is to have the parent on your team before you can help the child. Once the parent is established as a part of a team, the process of identifying problems and helping students adjust to school is expedited.

WHY TEAM BUILDING CAN BE SO HARD

While there are times when you are capable of resolving a disagreement with a parent, there are also times when you have tried and failed. When under pressure, you may not be able to be creative and flexible. These are the times when conflict begins to control a relationship. This could easily happen with Mr. Brown in the example earlier. He believes the school staff is angry with him and sees him as another disagreeable parent. Whether or not his daughter has a school adjustment problem is really not the issue here. But if she does, it will be much more difficult to learn what Mr. Brown knows about the problem if he remains angry and defensive.

The counselor presents an appreciation of Mr. Brown's point of view. If the counselor allows him to continue to feel that the school staff has no understanding of his intentions, a predictable battle of wills is forthcoming. Instead, Mr. Brown gets the message that the staff members are confused about his behavior, but are open to correcting their impression. This creates an atmosphere for openness.

One of the most difficult tasks we face as educators who are trying to help children with problems is to create an atmosphere of openness. This is especially difficult when the tendency is for conflict and dissension to dominate the relationship. Parents who have children with adjustment problems frequently are angry and blame the school. They may have tried to make the school deal with these problems for many years and failed. Regardless of who is to blame for the child's not improving, the parents may begin their relationship with you by presenting a blaming stance. While a situation like this may not feel fair to you, it is what you may have to face in many cases. It is an unfortunate reality that some students fail in school and the parents blame you. The problem of how to confront this issue is also an unavoidable reality. It deserves special attention in the discussion of how to help students with adjustment problems. The following sections provide you a variety of tools for dealing with this problem.

UNDERSTANDING CONFLICT

All of us experience conflict in our lives from time to time. These conflicts may vary from minor upsets to problems that occupy our thinking and behavior for extended periods of time. The process of teaching students and working with their families presents conflicts of various levels of severity. The way we think about conflict greatly influences how we attempt to solve problems. So let's take a fresh look at conflict.

Conflict is a powerful motivating factor in our lives. *Webster's Ninth New Collegiate Dictionary* defines conflict in a variety of ways.

> ... opposing action of incompatibles: antagonistic state or action (as of divergent ideas, interests or persons) ... mental struggle resulting from incompatible or opposing needs, drives, wishes, ... hostile encounter: **fight, battle, war** ... **collision.**[1]

According to this dictionary, it certainly sounds as if "conflict" is something we should want to avoid. Obviously we cannot. At least we cannot be totally free from "mental struggle and divergent ideas." But we can look at the differences people have from a different point of view. Conflict can motivate us to control future conflicts in a positive way and thus find a less painful and frustrating way to deal with an impasse.

How then does conflict, or the fear of an approaching conflict, motivate us? It attracts our attention and gives us a reason to want to take action. In addition, it brings us a stockpile of rich resources. As *Webster's Ninth New Collegiate Dictionary* points out, conflict involves interaction between divergent ideas or persons. The inherent diversity represented by any two potentially opposing persons or parties creates an opportunity to capture the best elements of each point of view and to combine them into a richer and more productive perspective.

Understandably, there are situations in the many spheres of our experience, both personal and political, where the potential for conflict will become a reality. But the point of this discussion is to argue that there are many other times when we appear headed for a battle that can be turned into a useful exchange of ideas. Ultimately these differences can be forged into a plan of action that benefits all parties involved. But how does one overcome differences when two parties are energetically motivated to stand up for their own point of view? This question must be initially addressed by examining how the way we think about and describe things contributes to conflict.

THE ROLE OF LANGUAGE IN CONFLICT

What goes on in our heads, our mental processes, is presented to the world around us by our language, according to Humberto Maturana.[2] There is a close relationship between the way we describe each other and the way we experience conflict. People who hear descriptions of themselves that allow them to feel appreciated and understood are less resistant to change. They are more likely to be open to the possibility of participating in the change process. But people who hear descriptions that they perceive as threatening their "subculture" can become *very* resistant.

SUBCULTURE AND CONFLICT

Subculture can be thought of as another person's particular point of view.[3] While being unique to that individual and highly idiosyncratic, it includes all the elements of subculture we normally consider, such as religion and race. But it also can be thought of as the very specific ways one looks at the world. This comes from many experiences, both past and present, conscious and unconscious. It includes values, old family practices, and thousands of other influences that lead to a way of perceiving events. Subculture can affect the way someone views a school system. For example, the previous experience parents have had with a school system creates an identity that influences all future interactions with schools. A parent may believe that schools are insensitive bureaucracies that ignore the needs of the individual. If she has challenged a school in the past and won the battle, her definition of herself as crusader against the ills of public education is strengthened, and she will bring a distinct predisposition to any future interactions she may have with school staff members—in this case, one destined to precipitate conflict. Conversely, a parent who is awed by the incredible resources and excellent skills of teachers in a school has a different subculture.

When parents bring their subcultures with them to meetings at school, they meet teachers and counselors, each with their storehouse of experiences with parents and definitions of themselves as professionals. A merging of subcultures commences.

During this merging, polarization can occur and produce conflict. Or a mingling of points of view can occur, contributing to cooperation and sharing of ideas. During initial contacts with us, families test us to determine how we might react to their idiosyncratic manner of dealing with schools. Whether conscious or unconscious, their first interaction with us represents a search to determine just how we will respond to them. Of course, this works in both directions, because we are anxious to learn how they will treat us too. Our responses to each other immediately begin to define and describe our subcultures.

> "Is Mrs. White one of those pushy parents? Does this teacher think I'm too forward and aggressive?"

> "Oh no! I hope this parent doesn't think I'm one of those lazy counselors. Mr. Smith seems so relaxed and laid-back ... I sure hope he can do something to help my daughter."

The process of formulating descriptions of one another and understanding subcultures is reciprocal and ongoing. If we believe a description about us is both inaccurate and rigid, we are prone to defend our identity and to demand respect for our "subculture." At such times conflict and resistance to change become further entrenched.

A firm belief that our perception of events is the right one reduces the possibility of a mutual exchange of information and increases the likelihood for defensiveness.

TRANSFORMING CONFLICT INTO COOPERATION WITH REDESCRIPTION

How many of us know of situations where a really angry and blaming parent has quickly and easily made a positive contribution to a child's program? Stop and think of how often this same parent has tied you up in unproductive and upsetting conferences. Consider the amount of time you have spent explaining yourself to your department chairperson, principal, or superintendent when the parent has complained. It only takes one or two experiences like this to convince you that this is not the part of teaching or counseling you want to do very often. Battling with the uncooperative parent is hard work and robs valuable time and energy from other tasks.

But how do you remain open when under attack? Most parents attack because they don't know any better. They are worried about their child and naive about how schools work and barge right in wanting to know "why my son can't spell better" or "why my daughter must be subjected to name calling in the halls." Your first reaction may be, "You idiot, every child misspells words occasionally, and who doesn't take a little abuse in the halls." The parent attacks, and you become annoyed. A conflict emerges.

But you can ignore the attack. You can't ignore the gesture the parent has made to initiate contact with the school, but you can decide to think of the initial attack in a different way. Think of it as an invitation to talk with you and do not accept the specific complaint as the only agenda. In almost all cases, parents who have children with adjustment problems have a much broader agenda than "how John spells" or "why Mary is called a nerd by other students." They are worried. By calling you, they are also demonstrating that they are committed to helping the child. What appears to be criticism of the school is usually a cry for help. Fighting over the details of their complaint is like arguing over who holds the fire hose while the house burns down.

Tell parents that, while you understand their concern about spelling (or whatever) and will discuss that with them, you do appreciate their taking the initiative to contact you about their child's school program. Explain to them that you too are committed to helping their student and need them to help you understand the child better.

What does this verbal intervention really do? It acknowledges the parent's presenting a problem (spelling) but broadens the issue to address the child's overall adjustment. This is accomplished by inviting the parent to give you additional information about how the child is responding to school. Now the parent is defined as a useful and committed person. The old definition of an angry, blaming parent is superseded by a new definition. With the new definition, a new relationship is possible.

Most parents are relieved when they realize that their old

and ineffective ways of dealing with the school have now ceased to function. They do not really want to fight and are pleased to be cast into a new role by the school. Their new role as the "expert on the child" is a valuable one for you. The parents know a tremendous amount about how the child behaves at home and in the neighborhood. You can acquire this knowledge without jeopardizing your role as the expert on classroom process. You also don't have to agree with the parent about their initial complaint. After you tell the parents what you do with spelling instruction, you can move into the new relationship that you have facilitated.

Redefining the parent in no way has to threaten the boundaries of your role as a teacher or counselor. It clarifies roles and places parents in an honorable role as consultants to the school about the area they know the most about—their particular child. The invitation to fight is easily superseded by an invitation to join forces and work on the same team.

MAKING A POSITIVE RELATIONSHIP WITH PARENTS

Defusing the opening assault from a disgruntled parent is difficult. It takes practice. Any time you can change the initial meaning of a parent's message, you increase the chances of shifting a negative interaction to a positive one. The following drill will help you begin to do this. Each parent who approaches the school with a concern has good intentions. The manner by which he or she approaches you, however, can make it very difficult to feel those intentions.

The Search for Positive Intentions

The first step in finding a new meaning for the behavior of someone you are upset with is to ask yourself the question: What are the possible motives or intentions a parent may have that would lead to the behavior you are seeing? Doing this requires you to place yourself in the parent's position and to attempt to view things from his or her point of view.

Let's Imagine

- What are they really trying to accomplish by meeting with me?
- What kinds of knowledge do they have about the school programs or my classroom?
- What pressures are they experiencing with their child?
- How does their opinion differ from mine?
- What are their real intentions and could any of these intentions be valid?

Pondering these questions can be thought of as a kind of mental calisthenics. Whether you discover the "right" answer is irrelevant. What matters is whether you have been able to consider *any* alternative possibility other than your initial one. By going through the "Let's imagine ... " steps, you are making a declaration about your state of mind. You are saying

> "I don't know! I am open to the possibility that there are hidden intentions that I have not been able to discover so far!"

The result is a mental openness that is a precondition for finding a positive meaning in their behavior.

The following example illustrates how a counselor might help an angry family to redescribe a teacher. Initially, Tom's father narrows down his opinion of the shop instructor very quickly to one word: "rigid." He then struggles to find a new way to think of the shop teacher:

> Tom comes home and complains that his shop teacher is unwilling to repeat his directions in auto shop. He quotes his instructor: "If you can't get it right with two explanations, then you're on your own." Tom's parents initially see his instructor as rigid and unhelpful. Then Tom's father remembers when he worked in a machine shop for a few years after he finished school. The shop foreman never repeated his instructions more than once. Anyone who became confused had to ask a co-worker or go find the foreman for clarification. Any time the foreman had to repeat himself, he was impatient and hostile. Tom's dad realizes that, while his initial

description of his son's shop teacher could be a valid one, he could also find an alternative meaning: "This teacher is preparing my son, whether he realizes it or not, for the real world of work. He is developing a more realistic set of expectations for the treatment he would be likely to receive if he ever finds a job in a commercial machine shop." From this realization, Tom's dad constructed a new description of the teacher as both a "wise" and "seasoned" instructor.

Now Tom's father can help him to experience the shop teacher in a different way.

Finding a New Description

Making a bridge from a negative meaning to a positive meaning is a difficult task and takes practice. The following drill will give you some practice at doing this.

Write a brief description of a parent who has approached you in an annoying or inappropriate way. Now reduce your description to several adjectives. The selection of one or two adjectives forces you to clarify your feelings about something and to put your description into a concise form. It also prepares you for the next exercise, which is designed to give you practice at stretching your initial opinion to include the possibility of other descriptions.

Instructions: Study each list of words and determine whether or not a person characterized by a word on list I could in any way also be characterized by a word on list II. For each match place the number of the characteristic from list II underneath the word on list I. You may place any number of words from list II under words in list I.

Here are some samples: Someone who is *naive* may also be *idealistic*. Someone who is *arrogant* may be *strong* and *independent*. People who are *irritating* may be *committed* to a cause. *Careless* people may *trust* you to take care of things.

Begin the exercise on the next page.

RESENTFUL	1. loyal
	2. generous
RESISTANT	3. wise
	4. helpful
SELFISH	5. considerate
	6. gentle
AFRAID	7. nurturing
	8. understanding
WITHDRAWN	9. committed
	10. perceptive
PASSIVE	11. industrious
	12. concerned
AGGRESSIVE	13. confident
	14. courageous
ABUSIVE	15. relaxed
	16. fair
DEVIOUS	17. determined
	18. honest
PESSIMISTIC	19. reliable
	20. trusting
IRRESPONSIBLE	21. trustworthy
	22. obedient
RIGID	23. humorous
	24. creative
INSINCERE	25. strong
	26. inspired
CONDESCENDING	27. consistent
	28. articulate
ARROGANT	29. energetic
	30. effective
JUDGMENTAL	31. optimistic
	32. sophisticated
OBNOXIOUS	33. empathetic
	34. idealistic
LAZY	35. sympathetic
	36. compassionate
DEPENDENT	37. supportive
	38. unique
ANGRY	39. thorough
	40. independent
BLAMING	
HOSTILE	
NAIVE	
CARELESS	

Once you have placed words together, develop an explanation as to why the match may be possible. By considering several ways to describe someone, you begin to stretch the ways in which you can experience that person. For example, Tom's father may have had the following rationale for describing the shop teacher as "wise" after initially describing him as "rigid." His explanation might be the following:

> "I have known a lot of people who seemed rigid. Sometimes, even when I came to know them better, their behavior resulted in unwise decisions and inflexibility. But some other people, who have initially seemed rigid, eventually began to look wise. They had developed a way of doing things based on past experience and knew the safest and most reliable method for accomplishing a task. Maybe Tom's shop teacher is basing his teaching style on experience and is really more wise than rigid!"

Playing this matching game is the second mental calisthenic for practicing the art of finding a positive meaning. Both exercises in this section should be used any time you find yourself in a situation where your initial description of a parent leaves you feeling angry and helpless. At such a time you may be blaming a problem on that parent instead of actively trying to discover a way to define him as a useful member of your team.

REDESCRIPTIONS MOST FREQUENTLY NEEDED BY TEACHERS AND COUNSELORS

Learning and refining ways to engage and work with families requires help from consultants trained in these areas. However, most of us who work in schools as teachers and counselors cannot spend a great amount of time with resource consultants to learn new techniques. We are educators, not family therapists or psychologists. It is therefore necessary to have some general guidelines for applying redescription in school systems.

1. Use the drills and exercises in this chapter even when you believe a situation is hopeless. Your willingness to try to do something different may give a message to a parent that you are open to other ways of experiencing them.

2. Use your professional support system to discuss the conflicts you face. Talk with colleagues, supervisors, and/or the school psychological consultants if you have them. Tell them what you are trying to do and ask for their ideas. Describing your approach to someone else also help you rehearse it and permits you to hear how it sounds. Revise what you want to say to a parent if you feel you need to.

3. Simplify your descriptions of parents, and act accordingly. You can think of aggressive, intrusive parents as "questioning parents." You can say the following to this kind of parent:

"I understand that you feel strongly about your child's program and that is why you have come into school so quickly to learn more. It is refreshing to have parents who take the time and initiative to come see us before problems or concerns become too large to handle. It's no good to let worries fester too long. If we don't know how you perceive the school process we lose a lot of valuable information that might help us help your child. I realize we might not agree on everything we discuss, but at least you are making it clear that you want to deal with the school in an honest and straightforward manner. I can really appreciate that. Now I understand you have some questions for me. Let's try to deal with them."

If you know you are about to deal with "questioning parents," give them this message as soon as you sit down with them or at the beginning of the telephone conference. Immediately let them know that you do not consider them aggressive or pushy. Redefine their behavior as inquisitive and their motives as honorable, that is, to "come into school to talk about problems before they become too great." Invite them into an interaction that does not blame them or let them maneuver you into a situation where they can force you to reject their style of interacting with you. Doing this will not necessarily make all future interactions wonderful, but it may contribute to a lessening of the tendency to slip into a full blown battle.

PASSIVE, WITHDRAWN PARENTS

You can think of passive and withdrawn families as "trusting." If you have tried to engage a withdrawn family and cannot, there is a tendency to think of them as negligent. Providing you do not have enough information to compel you to file a petition of abuse and neglect (see Chapter Fourteen), the only way to ensure a reasonable relationship with them is to redefine them. You can telephone or write and say the following:

> "I realize that it is difficult for you to come into school given all the demands on your time. (List a few if you know what they are.) But I know you want to keep informed about your son/daughter's school progress. We believe that students do better in school when their parents have information about their program. So I will forward you a report (specify how often) for you to look over. I know you are busy so if I don't hear form you I will trust that there are no major concerns or problems you want me to know about. If after reading the report you want to contact me for any reason, here's my telephone number. I appreciate your confidence in our school program and know if anything really serious comes up that you are the kind of parent who will contact me."

This message will not change a passive parent to an active one very often. But it will accomplish several things. Nothing is lost if they do not contact you. They know you will assume that they approve of the program. You have implied that you assume they are reading the report card or weekly report. If they don't read it, they know you have no way of knowing that and therefore will not judge them as negligent.

But your contacting them and offering information treats them as important members of your team. It defines them as monitors and may dispel their fears that you have judged them incompetent because they are not available. If they believe you have judged them this way, they may intentionally or inadvertently undermine your effort to help the student.

Redefining parents as "questioning" or "trusting" does not magically change them into cooperative resourceful members of your team. But it can alter negative interactions and in many cases give them a fresh start for working with a school system. If you can begin to describe them in a different way and contribute even slightly to a new identity, the possibility for creating a cooperative team is greater.

SUMMARY

Many attempts to help students become bogged down by cycles of mutual blame. Breaking the cycle of blame and drawing together a team of adults to support a student's adjustment to school is one objective of this book. Not all difficulties can be handled by trying to see a parent in a positive light and not all children with adjustment problems can be helped by the school. It is difficult to tell which ones might be helped and which ones might not. If you try, little damage can occur. The gesture to be open and to try to understand the parent's intention is frequently well received. But to perpetuate a battle, which is the alternative, is hard work and usually produces no winners.

Notes

1. *Webster's Ninth New Collegiate Dictionary* (Springfield, Mass.: G. & C. Merriam, Co., 1987), p. 276.

2. Maturana, Humberto R., "Biology of Language: The Epistomology of Reality," in G.A. Miller and E. Lenneberg (Eds.), *Psychology and Biology of Language and Thought: Essays in Honor of Eric Lenneberg* (New York: Academic Press, 1978).

3. The notion of resistance arising from a threat to subculture is presented in greater detail in Appendix B, *The Conceptual Framework for Redescription.*

8

Working in a Parent/ Teacher Team

In previous chapters of the book we have considered a wide range of adjustment problems and have presented various approaches for resolving these problems. In some cases one adult, either the parent or teacher, can provide an effective program for the student. Often, particularly for difficult school or family adjustment problems, more than one adult needs to be involved. Chapter Eight presents some methods for working in teams along with a sample case of a small collaborative team effort between a parent and a math teacher. The case initially describes how both teacher and parent are angry and blame one another for the student's poor school performance. It continues with an illustration of how each adult is able to move beyond the blaming stage and to work together to provide support for the student.

ADVOCATING FOR A TEAM APPROACH

Parents and teachers can work together in a number of ways. Each approach takes time and energy, some more than others.

There are times when you or the parent can work on the problem without each other's help. For example, if Ralph forgets his gym clothes, the parent may find it considerably easier to handle the problem within the family. On the other hand, there are times when you may be successful in helping a student by merely requesting that he or she come in after school.

Team approaches between parents and teachers are necessary when you have found that your isolated efforts have not been successful in getting the student to change behavior. When this condition occurs, it is time to begin to build a cooperative team.

At such times it is necessary to engage the parent in a manner that is straightforward and does not initiate a cycle of mutual blame. This chapter will help you to apply some of the ideas introduced in Chapter Seven as we explore ways to build collaborative working relationships with parents.

Approach 1. Simple Information Exchange

One simple way for you to begin to start working with parents is to exchange information. Most parents are delighted to know more about their child's performance in school. They will be much more open to maintaining contact with you if you can provide them information before a crisis situation develops. As soon as you are worried about your student, make a connection with the parents. Reach out to them and begin to build a team of concerned adults. Become partners in the process of gathering information.

Once the student has received a failing grade, building the team starts to become more difficult. Frequently, parents report that they wish they had known sooner that their child was not doing well. Polarization can occur more easily at this time. However, if you preempt this predictable response by inviting the parent to be part of the team who monitors progress, you may be able to avoid a conflict later. The program is strengthened if students are present when the parent and the teacher meet to discuss the monitoring system. By being a member of the parent-school team, students can help to negotiate the details of the plan. They may discover loopholes or point out ways that the monitoring plan could be improved. Most importantly, they witness the cooperative effort between their parents and teachers. This permits students to see a positive interaction between the adults working to help them. Students may leave a meeting with a sense of pride when their parents complete a successful meeting with teachers, even if the result of the meeting means that they will be scrutinized more tightly. If the student can collect and carry the information so parents and teachers don't have to, all the better.

> Craig's dad has arranged with the French teacher to sign a "monitoring sheet" each Friday *if* Craig has turned in the week's homework on time. It is Craig's responsibility to remind the teacher to sign the sheet after class on Friday. Craig knows he must take the sheet to school on Fridays, have it signed, and take it back home and place it in his dad's hand at dinner time.

This simple system requires very little work on the part of the father and the French teacher. The father has to check the sheet but *does not* have to bother trying to determine whether or not Craig has done his French homework adequately. The teacher has to take a few seconds to determine if Craig's homework has been turned in and a few more to sign the sheet.

If Craig's grades start to drop, his dad will probably not be surprised because it is unlikely that Craig can produce good homework grades and still fail the course. If that begins to happen, the French teacher and the father can alter the monitoring system to include other types of information. But what is more important, the teacher has made contact with the parent *before* Craig has put a lot of stress on the relationship. Students with adjustment problems always eventually stress the team of adults trying to help them.

Approach 2. The Parent/Teacher Conference

If a phone call and a weekly monitoring sheet do not help the student to do better in school, it is necessary to meet with the parent and to explore other options. When monitoring sheets do not work, there is a strong possibility that the student's adjustment problem is complicated enough to require careful analysis and discussion between you and the parent. If you can meet and tighten your program with the student, the team becomes stronger. You can help many students this way and simultaneously model for parents how to define target behaviors, develop a behavior management program, and gather critical information for the purpose of monitoring.

Unfortunately, many students with adjustment problems cannot respond to the program you arrange with a parent. The less successful we are in helping students change problem behaviors, the more likely their parents will begin to become discouraged and confused. It is at this time in your relationship that you can either "make it or break it." Engaging parents when they start to blame you is difficult. It is more difficult, however, to struggle with a student whose parents are either actively or passively fighting you.

Approach 3. Working with Parents Who Appear Unavailable

Some parents are restricted by work schedules or family responsibilities and are not able to contact the school often. Telephone them and say that you will send them information on a regular basis. Explain that they are not expected to contact you unless they are concerned about something. Tell them that if you do not hear from them, you will assume that you have their approval and support.

You have now placed them in the role of passive "supervisors." By taking the initiative, you help to dispel their conscious or unconscious fear that you really think they are incompetent or negligent. This does not necessarily make them more competent, but decreases the likelihood that they will undermine you. Occasionally, the new definition as "supervisor" helps them to become a little more active with the school. If they do not contact you very often, telephone them and say you appreciate their vigilance and confidence in you to handle things on your own. Ask them if they have detected anything at home that they think you should know about. If they have no suggestions, tell them that you are relieved that there are no problems and will continue with the present program.

Using these approaches with parents may appear to be too

time consuming. They would be if you had to use them with all your students. But students with adjustment problems have special needs. Attempting to meet those needs may become very time consuming. Approaching the parent and attempting to build a cooperative team with them may save you time in the future. Once you lose the parent, helping the child becomes more complicated. It is therefore important not to become trapped in a cycle of mutual blame.

BREAKING THE CYCLE OF BLAME

The following case study reveals a teacher and a parent who are initially angry with one another. But instead of allowing their negative feelings to escalate, the teacher is able to help the parent move beyond the initial stage of being angry and blaming the school for the problem. Eventually a well-coordinated team forms, and they develop a comprehensive plan to help Al.

> Al Duit is a 12-year old in the seventh grade. He comes from a well-adjusted family who believes in Al's education. Al did well in elementary school and entered the junior high with reading and math skills comparable to his grade level. Al is an active and excitable student who loves sports. He has lots of friends. Throughout his childhood, his parents' only complaint was that he tended not to follow directions and had to be told what to do over and over again. He always told them, "I'll do it later."

> Al's story begins near the end of the first quarter of his seventh grade school year. Mr. Duit had spoken to Al's teachers in September and asked them to let him know if Al was slacking off in any subjects. He had heard nothing and assumed all was going well. Al works on his homework each night, even if it is only for 20 minutes or so and told his parents that normally he completed most of it in study hall. About ten days before the end of the marking period, Al received a notice saying he was failing math. Mr. and Mrs. Duit were upset. How could this have happened?

> It happened because Al had not done either homework or classwork after the first four weeks of school. The teacher had neglected to call home because she believed that he would "shape up" all by himself once he received the failing

notice. The parents had no idea if the homework was being completed and never thought about math after the initial phone conference earlier in the term. Does this mean

Al is a bad kid?
Al's teacher is a poor teacher?
Al's parents are irresponsible?

No. It is quite normal for the teacher to overlook making that phone call when she has 25 other students in the class and a total of five classes a day. Certainly it would have been courteous for her to call, but it is understandable that she would forget. It does not make her a bad teacher any more than a parents' forgetting the student's dentist appointment on a hectic day makes them bad parents. These things just happen.

Al is not a bad kid. He understood his math the first few weeks of school during the review of last year's work. But, as a new student to the junior high school having to change classes, use a locker, and remember to have materials ready for different teachers, he became confused. He lost math worksheets, did not take notes, and, as a result, did not have sufficient information to do his homework each evening. He knew he was lost. Also, Al knew that a friend of his had to stop playing his fall sport because his grades had dropped. Because Al was the star on his football team, and he was afraid he would have to quit before the season ended, he convinced himself that he was doing all right in math and that he could make up the work he missed. He was wrong. He had no idea what was going on in math. Ten days before marks were due, Al owed the teacher 15 out of the 21 math worksheets, and he had failed three tests.

Now, Mr. Duit might want to call Mrs. Cosine, the math teacher, and say, "Why didn't you tell us what was going on sooner?" She might want to reply with, "I have 125 math students to worry about; why didn't you give me a call? You have only 1 to worry about."

If this were to happen, both parent and teacher will be convinced that the other is to blame. Each has made statements that imply that the other is not competent. Consequently, each person has posed a threat to the other. The result may be a loss of face, which can lead to a battle of mutual blame. This decreases the chances of the parent and teacher being able to work as a cooperative team to help the student. It is at this point in the relationship that the process of trying to work together will probably stop.

Resolving Angry Feelings About Parents

How do you move beyond the stage of being angry and blaming one another to the stage of building a cooperative team? The first thing to do is to deal with your anger and blame before you contact the parent. It is normal to feel angry if the parent has implied that you are not teaching properly. At such times you may wonder if the parent really just wants the school to take over all the responsibility of all the students' problems.

Step 1. Acknowledge Angry Feelings. Realize that most people have the tendency to blame someone or something else when they are attacked. You can vent these feelings with a friend or colleague. Not talking about them may cause you to become more upset and resentful.

Step 2. Prepare Yourself to Make Contact with the Parent. Refrain from being angry or blaming the parents for the problem. Try to visualize the situation from their point of view.

> You might visualize Al's parents' point of view this way: If I were Al's father, it is quite possible that I would not think I needed to check with the school a second time. He might think, "Al has been going to his room every night to study, and I assume he is doing some work. He has a study hall each day where he can also do some work. I think it's time, now that he is in junior high, that I trust him to get his work done on his own. He has to learn responsibility sometime."

After visualizing how the parent might view the situation, it is easier to imagine that your initial judgment may be too narrow. If you can see the possibility that the other adult was not incompetent and to blame for what happened, it is easier to make a telephone call and initiate the process of starting to work together.

Step 3. Try to Determine the Parents' Intentions. Why did the parents deal with Al as they did?

Mr. Duit could have believed that Al was old enough to begin to be trusted now that he was 12. Al told him his work was being done, and he had no reason to doubt him. There were no other adjustment problems to worry about, and the first part of the seventh grade was a good time to let his son know how much he respected and trusted him.

Of course, there are many possible ways one could imagine what intentions Mr. Duit might or might not have had. You are encouraged not to dwell upon whether any imagined or proposed intention is *true, false, right,* or *wrong,* but to realize that there are many possible ways to look at and to describe events. If you can imagine any potentially positive intention, you are mentally preparing yourself to conceive of positive ways to work on a team to help the student. Just realizing that it is possible to move beyond your initial anger and tendency to blame can make the next step in forming the team easier.

Step 4. Decide What You Will Say in Your Phone Call. How will you express your concern without implying blame?

"Mr. Duit, I am calling because I am concerned about your son's performance in math. I realize that it may be next to impossible for you to know whether or not he is preparing his homework each night, but I have not had an assignment turned in for some time now. I had hoped my reminding him weekly would make a difference, but he continues to seem unable to organize himself well enough to catch up. Could we meet sometime to discuss this problem further?"

Initiating contact in a nonblaming fashion can help to prepare the parent for the process of building a cooperative team approach to the student's problems. By broadening your point of view to consider the other's position, you begin to become aware of his perspective on the problem. This is a good first step in working together.

It also serves as a first step to communicating to the student that you do not blame him. It is predictable that Al wonders if you blame him because he is not doing well in school. When Al hears that his teacher called home to arrange a meeting to discuss how he "organizes himself in math," a specific meaning is attached to the upcoming meeting. This specific message from Mrs. Cosine can also help eliminate Al's fantasy that he is considered "bad" or "lazy." It tells Al that Mrs. Cosine is not angry at his dad for not "making him do his homework." Even if Mrs. Cosine has not implicitly or explicitly stated these negative messages, Al may fear she believes them unless she explicitly states otherwise.

Step 5. Schedule a Meeting to Gather Specific Information About the Student's Difficulty. Schedule the meeting at a time when students can attend. There is a natural tendency to meet without students present because adults frequently believe it will be easier to talk openly about the students if they are not there. But the benefits of having them members of your team outweigh the difficulties in most cases. Teachers and counselors may have to struggle to phrase their descriptions more tactfully if students are in the room, but this rarely detracts from the meeting. The process of struggling to find a way to describe students in an objective and non-blaming way positively contributes to the process. As students witness the way teachers and counselors respect and collaborate with their parents, they can develop a sense of pride. By seeing how mom or dad look better in the eyes of the school and how their teachers are supported by their parents, students are removed from a loyalty bind. A loyalty bind is a situation in which students believe that their parents are right for blaming the school for failures, while simultaneously wanting to perform well for those teachers. If they do well in school, they prove their parents wrong; if they prove their parents correct, they fail in school. This is why it is crucial for students to be at the school-family meeting and to observe their parents and teachers working together on a collaborative plan.

It is very important to have a structure prepared for the meeting. The parent does not know how to run family-school meetings, so it is your responsibility to chair the meeting in a way that can potentially help the student. Parents who are upset with their child's school performance have the tendency to monopolize meeting time by *either* blaming the school staff or their child for the problems. Usually they criticize the school. In either case, allowing them just to complain or criticize will not help the student.

CONDUCTING A STRUCTURED
FAMILY-SCHOOL MEETING

There is a natural tendency, in lieu of not knowing what else to do, to allow the meeting with the parent to consist of little more than a continuous reporting of the student's symptoms. Frequently, the symptoms that are reported imply blame, and the meeting escalates into a battle of "who's to blame" for the student's school adjustment difficulties. Without a clearly defined structure, most meetings with upset parents will deteriorate to this state. *You* must prevent this from happening. Structure the meeting by allocating portions of time for the following phases of the conference.

Stating the Problem

If you have 45 minutes available to meet, allocate 10 to 15 minutes for all the members of the group to describe how they understand the problem. The parents and students must be included as one of the reporters. A minute and a half of carefully prepared description can say a tremendous amount about a student's behavior. It is unnecessary to repeat descriptions of symptoms. If more than one staff member sees the behavior that is being reported, all you have to do is to agree with that reporter and then add any unreported and unique information.

Ask the parent to give a brief description of the student's difficulty. The example you and other teachers set will help the parent to know how the meeting is run. If the parent or another teacher begins to report redundant materials, just to complain or to blame the school, firmly, but politely interrupt. Explain to the group that you appreciate their candor and commitment to reporting as much information as they can, but it is very important to move onto the next stage of the meeting. Point out that you have been given ample information about the student's problem and cannot solve all the problems at one time. Emphasize that you believe the best way to work together to help the student is to focus on a few target behaviors at a time. Finally, stress that you must begin developing an appropriate plan of action and you will need the rest of the meeting time to do that.

Mrs. Cosine makes a clear and concise summary of what the team has reported: "O.K. From what you've told me, Al seems to have problems in the following areas:

1. He doesn't seem to listen to classroom presentations.

2. He doesn't take notes or complete the classroom worksheets.

3. His homework is seldom completed when he turns it in, which is only about half the time.

With the three target behaviors listed, you have established a realistic agenda for the remainder of the meeting and, it is hoped, structured the discussion away from chronic complaining about the problem. Chronic complaining easily turns into chronic blaming. Assume that most parents (or teachers) do not really want to spend an entire meeting just complaining, particularly if they can be drafted into a role of helping to plan a treatment program.

Evaluating Information

Decide what the student must do *first* before things can get better. Ask each member of the group to give you their opinion. Emphasize the importance of gaining the perspective of all members; student, parent, teacher, and/or counselor. Select one "target behavior" that the student needs to do before other tasks can be completed.

Al must learn to take accurate notes before he can:

1. Do the classroom worksheets.

2. Complete homework assignments adequately.

3. Get better test grades.

Developing a Plan of Action

Define the target behavior in clear behavioral terms. Decide exactly what it is you want the student to do.

"We want Al to listen to his teacher and write down the notes she gives. This means copying the examples off the board and recording what she says when she is explaining the problem."

Developing a Monitoring System

It is important to be able to tell if the student does what you have asked. An adult must observe the target behavior to determine this. Choose an adult who has enough knowledge of the behavior to judge whether or not he has complied with the learning contract.

Mrs. Cosine might look at Al's notebook at the end of each week to make sure he is taking accurate math notes. But Al needs to take it to her without being reminded. The parent would have no idea whether or not the notes were any good, so it is preferable for Mrs. Cosine to check the notebook.

Determining Roles

It is crucial to know whether or not each member of the team realistically has time to do what you have decided. Some parents will offer to play a role. This is much more likely to happen if they have started to feel that you perceive them as respected and valued members of the team. Your skill in moving the meeting toward resolution of the problem and away from blaming will encourage parents to perceive themselves as necessary, useful, and active team members. Some parents, however, will simply not have the psychological or social resources to play an active role. You do not want them to feel that, by default, they are not helping with the student's program. Once you determine a parent is unlikely to participate actively, assign them the role of monitor. Explain to them as the new program starts, that their child may react differently at home. Ask them to watch for any signs of stress or changes in emotional status. Tell parents that you consider their observations to be extremely valuable bits of information. Encourage them to call you any time they have noticed something they think you should know. Tell them that if you have not heard from them that you will assume everything is all right. In this manner, no matter what they do you have not defined them as incompetent. Parents who believe we think they are incompetent are more likely to try to perceive us as incompetent.

Returning to our case about Al, Mrs. Cosine might get the parent to volunteer to play an active role:

> Al's father might suggest to Mrs. Cosine: "If you can't always check Al's notes during class, tell him to drop by after school for a few minutes so you can look them over. We will tell him he has to do this, even if it means going to sports practice a little late. We will check with him after school Friday to see if he has checked with you."

Now the parent is an active team member and can support a behavior that Mrs. Cosine can monitor. This is the time during the parent meeting when the team of adults begins to believe that they really can have a positive impact on the student's behavior. Positive momentum is established, and with it, a useful building block for future interactions. Each time you can engage a parent in a specific and productive program to help the child, it increases the chances that you can do it again, even if matters appear to be worse in the future.

Involving the Student

This step brings up the question of the student's role in the planning of a program. Any time parents and teachers are comfortable having the student present at family-school meetings, that student should be invited to attend. Rarely are there reasons why the student should not attend and there are always reasons why they should. Some of these reasons are the following:

- Many students will show behavioral improvements once they witness the concern and effort that their parents and teachers are investing into their school programs. By being in family school meeting, students can observe the teamwork between their parents and their teachers. Seeing their parents treated by teachers and counselors as important and credible team members is very important. The school and parents appear to be in concert with the plan to help students. Consequently it is less likely that they will attempt to manipulate either party and more likely to believe that they can adjust to school without jeopardizing loyalty to the family. Loyalty conflicts are avoided when students believe their parents and teachers agree on what would help them the most.

- A well-run meeting is a contracting session. Problems are outlined, resources allocated, and agreements discussed. The sooner the student is included in this process the more likely he is to begin to take responsibility for his own behavior.

- Many students make valuable contributions. They see their adjustment problem from a different perspective. This allows them to offer information no one else could contribute. When a contract is discussed, the student can be extremely useful at pointing out loopholes and oversights.

- Before students can be placed on a program that involves positive consequences or rewards, it is crucial to have the student tell you what they are motivated to work for.

- Finally, students must know what role they must play. You should put the student in charge of passing the information between parent and school as often as possible. Most students, if properly motivated, take a monitoring sheet home on a daily or weekly basis.

This is how the entire plan might sound when it is explained to Al by his father:

"Al, we are going to start a program with your math teacher, Mrs. Cosine, to help you bring up your math grade. The first step is to get you to take better notes, so you understand the material. You must copy examples from the board and take notes when she explains the problems. Two times a week she will check your notebook to see if you have an accurate and complete set of notes. If she can't do this during class, she will ask you to come in after school for a few minutes. On Fridays, as outlined in your contract, you will go up to her after class and give her your monitoring sheet. If your notebook has been acceptable, she will sign the sheet. It is your responsibility to remind her to do this, not hers. If you forget, that's not a good excuse, and your contract spells out what will happen!"

Mrs. Cosine does not have to remember to find Al or to get to a phone to call the parent. This program may not work, but if it does, it is the simplest method to use. If the adults have to be responsible for gathering information, it will be harder to do because daily schedules sometimes interfere. We want the responsibility to be the student's, not yours. We also want the flow of information to be as consistent as possible. Either you or the parent can set up a system of rewards and restrictions.

Example of a parent-initiated program: "Al, until you can show us you are doing a little better job in math class, we are going to restrict your television. From now on there will be no T.V. week nights (that includes Sunday through Thursday nights) unless you get Mrs. Cosine to sign your feedback sheet saying you took accurate notes. You must get the sheet back, and give it to your mother or me. So even if you take good notes and forget to get her to sign the monitoring sheet or lose it on the way home, there will be no T.V."

Example of a teacher-initiated program: "Al, if you can turn in good notes for two weeks in a row, you will earn an extra 15 minutes of free time."

This system involves a minimal amount of parent and teacher time. Once the program is set up, which does require a meeting at school, the teacher only needs to check the notes several times a week and sign the monitoring sheet when the student reminds him. The parents must be sure to ask for this monitoring sheet and to maintain consistently the structure they have agreed upon in the contract. The "burden of proof" is on the student, where it should be. It is part of his education to both learn math and to be accountable and responsible. These are things he will need to know how to do when he leaves school. This system of having the student do most of the work offers him a rich learning opportunity. If the parent or his teacher did this for him, it would limit Al's opportunity to develop responsibility. At the same time Al is given enough structure and assistance to deal with the stress and pressure of a school problem that he obviously could not handle alone.

The steps taken so far may be all that is necessary to help a student like Al. However, some students cannot be helped without taking additional steps. The discussion of the parent/teacher team continues with steps that can be used for a wide variety of additional problems. Because Al is a familiar character he will continue to be our subject.

After Al learned to take good notes, he still needed to work on completing in-class worksheets, going in after school for extra help, and completing homework each night.

Finding Another Target Behavior

Selecting a second target behavior is a good way to continue the program once Al has accomplished the first one. Continue the process until your general goal has been met. In this way Al's parents and teacher help him to pay better attention in class and then add new specific target behaviors until he is regularly achieving several academic objectives. They might expect him to take good notes, complete all classroom and homework assignments, and get a grade of "C" or better before Mrs. Cosine signs his sheet. His parents should proceed gradually to this point, and Al will probably make his contract by achieving all the target behaviors that his teacher and parents identified when they initially detected his problem with math. On those weeks that he does not meet the conditions of the contract, it would be appropriate for the structure of "no T.V." to be in effect.

Strengthening the Reinforcers

If one consequence doesn't motivate the student to achieve the objective on the contract, other consequences can be added. Al's parents decided that they would limit restrictions to no television and no trips to the mall if it became necessary. They decided against restricting him from extracurricular activities, the Boy's

Club, and outings with the family, even if those included going to the movies.

One of the hardest things to do is to be consistent in disciplining. Students are masters at convincing teachers and parents to make exceptions and loosen up. Rarely will this help the student to accomplish the behavioral goal you have set. If a restriction doesn't work initially, make sure the student is not gaining some reward from it that may not be obvious to you.

If you have instituted all the appropriate restrictions you can think of and the problem persists, additional services may be needed.

Chapter Ten, Adding Regular Education Support Services, presents a discussion of an expanded team approach. Additional help may be needed for students with problems that have persisted after parents and classroom teachers have done all they could. Many students can be helped through the use of the parent/teacher team. If the student changes his behavior and begins to perform in school, then you have solved a problem in a reasonably simple way. However, if the student has not responded to your parent/teacher team, then he may have a more complicated adjustment problem and, consequently, require a different solution. By now you have gathered valuable diagnostic information. This information will be extremely useful to the members of the school's guidance or special education department, with whom you can construct a comprehensive team approach.

9

Meeting the Team of Special Players

As you go through the process of identifying problem students and developing treatment programs, it will become obvious which students continue to experience adjustment problems. Even if you are successful at involving the parent, some students will require additional services. The remainder of the book deals with the treatment of moderate to serious adjustment problems. This always requires your working on a team with other professionals in your schools and frequently in the community. Chapter Nine presents brief descriptions of the various professionals you may need to work with as the team to help the student grows larger and more complicated. Having a clear understanding of their roles and how you might use their particular expertise is the first step in becoming an effective team member.

A WHO'S WHO IN PUBLIC SCHOOL PERSONNEL

Adjustment Counselor: A school adjustment counselor may perform a role very similar to that of the school social worker (to be discussed shortly). Adjustment counselors focus their time primarily on school students who are both underachieving and having adjustment problems. They provide a liaison among parents, teachers, and administrators, and they support students directly by working with them either in counseling or in the classroom.

Attendance Officer: The school has the responsibility of investigating the cases of students who do not come to school on a regular basis (ten days consecutively, for example). An attendance officer (sometimes called truant officer) is employed to locate truant students, visit the home, and interview the parent and student. A report is then submitted by the attendance officer to the school administration. If the absence is due to illness, the school can determine if the student is eligible for academic support during this illness. But if the student is truant (not ill, but not attending school), most states require the school to petition the local district court for assistance. The attendance officer assists the school in the process of presenting the case of the truant student to the judge. If the judge determines that the student is truant, he or she may direct the District Court Probation Department to provide supervision or services for the student. As a preventive treatment, the attendance officer may explain to a student and family what they can expect in court if truancy continues. Many states emphasize providing services to students who are truant rather than punishing them. These services might include court-monitored curfews, referral to individual or family therapy, or referral to a local community mental health facility for a social/psychological evaluation.

Bilingual Education Teacher: This teacher may be available in schools for students whose native language is not English. He or she provides classroom instruction in the student's native language.

Chapter I Instructor: The federal government provides funds to schools for the purpose of providing extra remedial help for students who function below grade level in the areas of reading or mathematics. The Chapter I instructor is responsible for screening, testing, and teaching students who have a grade-level equivalency approximately one to two years below their age level and generally score at the fortieth percentile or lower on standardized tests. The remedial education they provide is designed to improve basic skills and to teach the student the skills he needs to function on a level equivalent to his current grade. Chapter I staff also teaches students study skills, learning strategies, and consults with the regular classroom teachers on methods to use with students who have problems with basic skills.

Developmental Pediatrician: Although few schools traditionally use the services of this specialist on a regular basis, it is important to understand his or her role in helping school students. A developmental pediatrician specializes in assessing the student's physical and neurological development. Each student is evaluated in comparison to the level of functioning expected of normal students of the same age. If, for example, parents or teachers believe a student has a delay in the development of coordination, they should seek the advice and support of the school nurse, special education director, and/or family doctor to investigate the possibility of an evaluation with a developmental pediatrician.

Director of Special Education: The director of special education (SPED director) is the school administrator responsible for the delivery of services to all the district's students who have special education needs. This person's role is to supervise the process of referring, screening, evaluating, and educating students eligible for special services. In addition, the director of special education prepares the special education budget, hires and supervises staff, and facilitates the resolution of conflicts parents may have with the way services are being provided to their students. The special education director is the primary person responsible for record keeping and providing the state and federal governments with the information they require to monitor the delivery of services and to financially reimburse each district for a portion of its costs. Parents or teachers can consult this administrator with questions about the state and federal special education laws and appeal to him or her for assistance in solving difficult problems or disagreements about services students are receiving.

English as a Second Language Instructor: The ESL instructor provides non–English-speaking students with instruction in English. Schools with a specified percentage or number of students who cannot speak English are required to provide such instruction.

Guidance Counselor: Schools employ guidance counselors to schedule classes (secondary level) and to provide counseling and support to the student body. They also work in teams with the classroom instructors to assist students with academic problems. The guidance counselor can be a primary contact for parents and can act as a manager of information and special programs. For example, meetings between parents and teachers to solve a student's social adjustment problem might be organized and chaired by the counselor. In addition, at the secondary level guidance counselors help students choose their courses and make schedule changes. They also are available to provide individual or group counseling sessions and deal with a wide variety of concerns, including occupational-educational information for postgraduate placement, study skills, information on drug or alcohol abuse, adjustment to personal problems, and discussions involving peer pressure and school social atmosphere. If a student needs additional help beyond that which the parent or regular education teacher can provide, the guidance counselor acts as a referral agent and can provide information about tutorial programs, special education, and counseling outside of the school.

Language, Speech, and Hearing Specialists: Sometimes called speech/language pathologist, the LSH specialist is trained to evaluate a student's ability to understand and express ideas effectively and to speak clearly and fluently. Adequate hearing is a prerequisite for effective speech and language development. When students are identified as having problems in these communication areas, they qualify for special education services. LSH staff offer services that have a wide variety of applications. They help students with hearing losses learn to develop effective means of understanding and expressing themselves. The speech/language therapy they provide not only helps students to speak smoothly and clearly, but also to organize their thoughts before speaking. They also work with students who hear and speak adequately, but who find difficulty comprehending spoken and/ or written language. If a student appears to be delayed in any aspect of communication such as hearing or gathering and using information, the parent or regular education teacher should ask the district's LSH specialist for a preliminary consultation to determine if a more formal evaluation process should occur.

Learning Disabilities Specialist: An LD specialist is a certified special education teacher who works out of a resource room or consults other teachers in their individual classrooms. The primary focus of these specialists is on the student's ability to gather and process adequately both verbal and computational information and to express their thoughts in verbal or written form. Students with learning disabilities have an impaired ability to gather and use information effectively in the regular classroom setting. For example, some students cannot comprehend material presented orally; others do not learn as well from graphic or visual presentations; still others may need information presented in a concrete step-by-step manner before they can be successful in completing some academic tasks. LD specialists help students to develop alternative strategies for learning and coping with the demands of the classroom. They may provide remedial instruction using alternative teaching methods and equipment and help students develop and use special problem-solving techniques. Parents or teachers who have questions about a student's learning style or ability to take advantage of the traditional large-group, verbally oriented teaching approach may want to consult with an LD specialist. If a special education referral is made, LD personnel may be assigned the task of doing a formal learning disabilities assessment.

Nurse: The nurse offers emergency health care and treats minor health problems. He or she helps to decide whether or not a sick student should be sent home or to a physician for treatment. School health aides are directly responsible to the nurse.

The school nurse is an integral member of the pupil personnel services team as he or she gathers valuable information from visits a student makes to the nurse's office, from parents, and from medical assessments for special education evaluations. When schools conduct vision and hearing screenings, the nurse is responsible for the organization, supervision, implementation, and follow-up for these procedures. He or she usually has contact with most students in the school at one time or another. The school doctor's time is frequently managed by the nurse's office, which arranges schedules for sports physicals and consultations with staff on medical issues.

Occupational Therapist: Occupational therapists work with students who have an impaired ability to perform various specific physical tasks. These tasks may include hopping on one foot, catching a ball, or doing one sit-up. Their therapy focuses on both strength and coordination, and the primary goal is to train students to do the same kinds of physical tasks that students of the same age normally do. Occupational therapists frequently employ special equipment and devices to aid in their instruction. Parents of students who have been diagnosed as having developmental problems may want to investigate whether or not the school can provide occupational therapy services. Both the family pediatrician and the school's special education administrator are good resource people with whom to consult to begin this process.

Physical Therapist: The physical therapist is a specialist who works with students who have physical disabilities, muscle tone, and/or flexibility problems. They provide physical therapy a prescribed number of times a week and attempt to help students develop the strength and coordination necessary to function adequately in school and in the community.

Principal: The school principal is, in most schools, the head administrator of the school. He or she oversees the academic program, disciplinary procedures, and the overall operation of the school. Depending upon the size of the school, principals are assisted with their duties by a variety of other staff members. An assistant principal frequently handles school disciplinary matters and may be the first person to contact parents if a problem arises. Assistant principals, department heads, and/or curriculum coordinators assist with the development and management of the academic program and with the supervision of classroom teachers. The clerical support personnel in the principal's office usually know which staff member a parent or classroom teacher should contact first for help.

Even though schools have different ways of delegating tasks, the principal's office is a source of help for a number of concerns. Here is a sample list of the issues or problems that may be addressed to the principal or his or her designee:

> Management of classrooms, halls, and buses
>
> Comfort and safety of the building
>
> Policies and procedures for regular and special education
>
> Crisis or emergency situations
>
> Teacher or parent suggestions or complaints
>
> Participation on parent advisory groups or on teacher subcommittees

Psychiatrist: Larger school systems may have the consulting services of a psychiatrist, who is a medical doctor with a specialty in the diagnosis and treatment of psychological problems. The psychiatrist is used to help staff identify students with serious psychological problems and who may need special treatment either within the school or in a mental health facility in the community. They may also provide in-service educational training to members of the pupil services staff to help them learn to recognize and deal with specific psychiatric problems. If a school staff member discovers a student in a severe psychological crisis, the psychiatrist could be called upon to facilitate a placement in an appropriate hospital or residential treatment facility.

Psychological Consultant: Some larger schools contract the part-time services of a psychologist to consult with their staff members about students who have emotional problems. There are several kinds of professionals who may provide these consultations, for example, psychiatrists, who have a medical doctor's degree (M.D.) plus special training in psychiatry; a licensed clinical psychologist, who has a Ph.D. in psychology; a licensed clinical social worker, who has an M.S.W. degree; and a counseling psychologist, who has a doctorate in education (Ed.D.) and a state certificate to assess and treat people with psychological problems. Each of these professionals has been trained to assess and treat psychological problems. They assist school staff members through the use of clinical consultation meetings during which various treatment approaches are reviewed and discussed.

Resource Room Teacher: Departments of special education employ teaching specialists trained to work with students who have a variety of special education needs. They work with students who have been found to have learning problems and require help beyond the regular school program. Resource room teachers provide special curriculums, remedial instruction, tutoring, monitoring, counseling, and case management and serve as a parent liaison. Their roles vary according to the kind of problems their students have, and they may work with students for one academic period a day up to the entire day depending upon the severity of the student's needs. Regular education teachers and parents need to work in teams with the resource room teachers to maintain good communication and a consistent approach. Resource room teachers can help you to develop additional learning activities to supplement and reinforce what is being taught in the special education classroom.

School Committee/Board of Education (Local Education Authority or Local School Board): Each local education association is governed by a group of elected officials whose primary role is to set policy, establish the budget, and supervise the superintendent of schools. While you normally have your issues and concerns represented for you by the school administration, there are times when they may want to have direct contact with the school committee/board. A particularly appropriate time to have direct contact is when budget hearings are occurring. Parents and teachers can express their views about specific programs or practices to the superintendent during this period of time. The school committee/board is the primary link between the city or town and the body of parents, teachers, and students. It is their responsibility to balance the interests of the local taxpayer with the need to provide an adequate public education for the students in the district.

School Physician: Some school systems have the services of a pediatrician or other physician on a limited basis. His or her role is to do physical exams for students who play sports, to consult with the nurse, and in some cases, to act as a liaison to other local doctors or clinics. The school physician might consult with the staff on screening, referring, and dealing with students who have special health problems.

School Psychologist: School psychologists support the guidance and special education departments by providing psychological assessments and counseling to students. They are trained to test students to determine their degree of mental ability and level of psychological functioning. If learning or neurological disabilities interfere with a student's ability to perform in school, the psychologist usually finds some indication of this problem on the battery of tests he or she administers. The psychologist also screens for psychological problems that may be affecting the performance of the student in school. During counseling the school psychologist does an informal screening of the student's emotional and academic level of functioning. If a problem is identified, a referral can be made for further assessment or help. Psychologists also consult with parents and teachers to formulate plans to help students do better in school. In some schools they help coordinate the services of a consulting psychologist or psychiatrist by organizing and chairing staff meetings with consultants and teachers.

School Psychometrist: Schools that are required to perform a large number of special education assessments sometimes hire a specialist called a psychometrist to do their testing. This specialist is trained to administer and interpret tests dealing with the student's level of academic functioning. Tests dealing with the student's psychological level of functioning are administered by the school psychometrist.

Social Worker: Some school systems hire social workers to assist with various tasks, including working with students who have emotional or psychological adjustment problems, doing assessments, consulting with staff, and working with families. The social worker might be assigned the task of performing the home assessment for the student's special education team meeting. During a home assessment, a family history is taken and the concerns and ideas of the family are recorded for presentation at the upcoming meeting in school. In addition, the social worker might provide counseling to students or facilitate school/family meetings. Some social workers are used to consult with staff members who work with students who have serious emotional problems or special needs.

Superintendent of Schools: The superintendent is the chief executive of the school district and has the ultimate responsibility for all the operations of the school. His or her primary role is to interpret the needs of the school to the school committee (or board) and to advocate for the policies and resources needed to operate the school's programs. Parent or teacher contact with the superintendent is usually limited to situations where other school officials cannot deal with a specific question or concern.

Therapeutic Day Program Staff: A few public schools offer special education programs in separate facilities for students with moderate to serious social and/or emotional adjustment problems. If these problems seriously limit the student's ability to make use of the traditional classroom setting, he or she may be referred to a therapeutic day program. These programs are located either in a nearby facility or in an isolated wing of the regular building and generally provide a full-day special program for students. They are staffed by certified special education teachers who specialize in working with students who have emotional problems and/or serious learning problems. Programs in separate facilities can provide students with a different schedule, highly structured small-group instruction, intensive counseling, and powerful behavior management programs. Therapeutic day program staff work simultaneously on student's academic weaknesses and the social/emotional problems that have caused them to do poorly in the regular school setting. If parents or teachers believe that a student is not responding adequately to his or her present special education services, it would be appropriate to consult the special education director and explore the possibility of a therapeutic day program, if it is offered by your school system. Commonly, students who need a full-day therapeutic program seem to be the kind of students who elude the services of other programs, either through manipulation or passive avoidance of tasks. (The sketches in Chapter One outline various types of social/emotional problems and will provide you with a more complete description of the kinds of problems that might merit a referral to a therapeutic day program.)

A WHO'S WHO OF COMMUNITY AGENCY PROFESSIONALS

There are also a wide variety of human resources in the community. As you encounter students in your school system who have serious adjustment problems or require special education, agencies outside the school may become involved in the student's treatment plan. In some cases, parents require treatment in the form of family therapy before the child can be helped with school problems.

Many communities, depending upon their size and location, have the following human services specialists who are available to the parent and school system. These professionals represent a rich resource of services that traditionally are not offered by the school system. If your community does not have some of the professional services listed earlier, they usually can be found either in the nearest metropolitan area or university town.

The range of possible services that are available to a student with a problem is immense. The following brief descriptions provide an introduction to the roles and services various agency staff members and private practitioners offer. The best way to learn more about their services and how they might be helpful to you is to call their office and request additional information.

Community-Based Outreach Worker: A few states have programs to help provide supervision and tracking of students on a 24-hour basis. Frequently, this outreach and tracking service is assigned to students who have behavior problems and is paid for by the department of social services, the department of youth services, or a district court probation department. The purpose of the service is to provide comprehensive supervision to students who have behavior problems and/or refuse to attend school. For example, if a student is truant from school, ignores a court-imposed curfew, is uncooperative with parents, or has problems in the community, the outreach worker becomes involved. He will attempt to locate the student and take him to an appropriate place. At such a time, the student is either returned home or to school. Students who have been extremely disruptive may be taken to a short-term detention setting. While maintaining custody, the outreach worker contacts the school and other agencies that are involved with the student and attempts to formulate a plan to help prevent a similar incident from occurring. The comprehensive, 24-hour supervision that they provide may be the only way to control some students who are beyond the control of the parent and school. Community outreach work is a preventive treatment designed to support students and their families. One primary goal is to prevent incarceration or repeated offenses for youth who have been released from a detention setting. Both parents and school officials should investigate this service if they are confronted with a student whom they are unable to control. If no such service exists in their community, the local district court probation department should be consulted. They may be able to provide similar services on a limited basis.

Certified Clinical Psychologists: Clinical psychologists have received a Ph.D. in psychology and are usually eligible for state licensing as psychotherapists. They may provide individual, group, and family therapy depending on their interests and specialities. They frequently provide psychological assessments. Many Ph.D. clinical psychologists also teach in universities and work as consultants to schools, hospitals, or mental health centers.

Community Mental Health Agency Staff: Community mental health centers employ a variety of professional staff members to provide psychological services to their clients. These professionals include psychiatrists, clinical psychologists, counseling psychologists, clinical social workers, drug rehabilitation specialists, and family therapists.

The services that these centers provide may include psychological assessment and evaluation; assessment of families; play therapy for students; individual, group, and family therapies; drug and alcohol rehabilitation counseling; and consultations with other agencies and schools. The comprehensive nature of the services offered by community mental health agencies provides the public with some advantages that the private therapist may not be able to offer. One advantage is the availability of a multidisciplinary team that can provide clinical supervision to each therapist. With the presence of a psychiatrist (M.D.), the use and management of medications can be addressed. Psychological test specialists can provide comprehensive assessments with information to help construct a thorough understanding of a client's problem. Finally, mental health centers accept Medicaid and health insurance payments. (Note: Many private therapists also accept insurance payments.) If funding through medical insurance is not available, in most cases a sliding scale is available to families according to their financial need. The relatively large staff, clinical supervision of therapists, and flexible fees make the local community health center a valuable resource for parents or teachers who are looking for a service that is not provided by the school.

Counseling Psychologist: Counseling psychologists have been trained in a school of education or in a department of psychology. The degree they receive varies according to the academic program and state certification regulations. Some counseling psychology programs lead to a doctorate; others do not. In many states they can become certified psychologists by passing a certification board exam and start private practices as psychotherapists. In some cases their background and training are similar to those of the clinical psychologist described earlier. Counseling psychologists may be trained in individual, group, or family therapy as well as mental health agency administration. Also they may work as staff members in mental health agencies or inpatient psychiatric hospital settings.

Developmental Evaluation Team Staff: In some areas local hospitals provide the services of a developmental team designed to provide a comprehensive evaluation of students with special problems. They offer a multidisciplinary team approach to identifying and assessing problems in the areas of psychological, social, educational, and physical functioning of the student. The staff consists of developmental pediatricians, psychologists, and educational assessment specialists and provides an additional source of expertise to the parent or educator who is struggling to understand the nature of a student's complex adjustment problem. A developmental team might be consulted for students who have serious learning disabilities, problems with coordination, and/or classroom behavior problems caused by lack of attention, distractibility, and impulsivity. School staff members who encounter parents who believe their child is not responding adequately to their school program can be advised to consult the special education director or their family doctor to seek a referral to the nearest medical center that sponsors a developmental evaluation team.

G.E.D. Instructor: The G.E.D. (Graduate Equivalency Diploma) instructor is an educator who offers classes to students who have left school before attaining a high school diploma, but who want to prepare for and pass their high school equivalency exam. These teachers provide instruction in the various subject areas tested on the G.E.D. exam. Classes are held in the evening in a local community college or high school. Each school's guidance department has information on the G.E.D. program. Parents of students who have dropped out of school have a valuable resource in the G.E.D. program if they want to reestablish the formal education process for their student.

Neuropsychologist: A neuropsychologist is a licensed psychologist who specializes in assessing the way the brain functions. His or her evaluations are designed to screen for learning disabilities or other neurological problems. Parents or teachers who are dealing with a student whose learning problem is not fully understood may want to investigate the possibility of a neuropsychological evaluation. Unless there is a severe impairment, this referral should be done after the school has made an effort to assess the student with their resources, that is, school psychologist and learning disabilities specialist. If the student continues to do poorly in school with special services, parents or teachers should seek the support of the director of special education or their family doctor for a referral. Neuropsychological evaluations are performed by community mental health agencies, by developmental teams at medical centers, and by licensed neuropsychologists in private practice.

Pastoral Counselor: Some members of the clergy provide psychological counseling services, for example, individual, group, and family counseling. Their training is similar to the training of a counseling psychologist, clinical psychologist, or clinical social worker. Families who have an affiliation with a church or synagogue and are in need of a counseling service should consult their minister, priest, or rabbi. They can either provide the service themselves or refer a family to a counselor.

Pediatrician: A pediatrician is a doctor who specializes in the treatment of children from birth to about age 17. He or she is one of the first professionals to consult when any kind of serious medical or psychological problem occurs. He or she can be helpful in deciding the next step in treating a student with either medical or psychological problems. Families who do not know where to find services can use the pediatrician as an advisor and a referral agent. Pediatricians are trained to screen students for problems in a wide range of areas and help parents decide when to use medical, school, or mental health services. Teachers, when working with parents who are confused about how to help their child and have exhausted the school's resources, recommend a consultation with the student's pediatrician.

Probation Officer: Probation officers are appointed court officials whose role is to manage and supervise the cases of court involved individuals. They may, in some circumstances, work on preventive programs to assist schools and families to help students before they need formal contact with the judicial system. Parents can consult the probation office of their local district court on an informal basis to arrange a meeting to familiarize the student with the law and probable consequences of breaking it.

Once the student is taken before a judge for truancy or for a more serious charge, probation officers assist in the management and supervision of that student until a disposition on the case has been made. At this time they may make recommendations to the judge, and then they will carry out the wishes of the court once the case is heard. The judge may order supervision in the form of curfews or consequences in the form of community service work. In more serious cases he or she may order an evaluation by a community mental health center or detainment in a secure setting for observation or evaluation. The probation officer supervises the student and the completion of any action the judge may have ordered. He or she also coordinates with other social service agencies. If a student has been sentenced to a youth services facility or detention center, the probation officer may help a youth services worker supervise the student's return to the community.

School students who are court involved will be served best if both the school staff and the parents maintain a strong cooperative relationship with the probation officer. He or she is potentially a valuable member on the educational/psychological treatment team.

Psychiatrist: A psychiatrist is a medical doctor whose specialty is the treatment of psychiatric problems. (A discussion of the role of a psychiatrist in the school system was presented earlier.) Psychiatrists work in a variety of roles in the community. Some are medical directors of psychiatric units in hospitals; others provide consultations to mental health centers; most provide psychiatric treatment (individual, group, or family therapy) either through a private practice or an affiliation with an agency or treatment center. The psychiatrist is a highly trained human services professional who has completed four years of college and up to seven additional years of medical school and internship. He or she deals with all aspects of psychological illness, although many develop specialties. If treatment requires the use of medications, the psychiatrist is the only psychotherapist licensed to write prescriptions. Parents who have students with serious problems may be referred to a psychiatrist by their family physician, the school, a psychologist, or a member of the clergy.

Regional Education Office Staff: The department of education of each state divides their geographical areas into regions. Each area has a regional education office staffed by specialists who are responsible for supporting and monitoring the schools in their areas. They visit schools to perform audits to ensure that each district is in compliance with the state's educational policies and regulations. The regional office sponsors in-service training, provides technical assistance, and provides information on grants for teachers and administrators. Both regular and special education problems are handled by the regional office staff. For example, if a parent and a school cannot agree on appropriate special education services for a student, the regional office provides a mediator. If the mediator cannot help the two parties come to an agreement, they conduct an appeals hearing and make a binding determination about the school's responsibility. Any questions parents or teachers have about the interpretation of their state's regular or special education laws can be addressed to the local regional education center staff.

Social Worker: Social workers (a discussion of the social worker's role as a school employee was presented earlier.) have different educational backgrounds and roles in the community. Social workers trained at the bachelor's degree level (four years of college) frequently work in social service agencies. They perform a wide range of services, including case management, counseling, family visitations, dispensing welfare funds, making foster care placements, referring clients to various other services, and acting as liaisons to schools or other agencies when it is necessary to arrange collaborative programs. Some develop specialties in investigating cases of suspected abuse and neglect; others work in emergency shelters, drug treatment programs, or half-way houses for people returning to the community from mental hospitals or correctional institutions. A social worker has a broad range of skills and contacts in the community. Parents and teachers can acquire information about the range of services in their community by contacting their state's local division of social services or welfare department.

Social workers trained at a master's degree level (more than four years of college education) are trained in psychotherapy and can become licensed or certified by their states as "clinical social workers." Along with psychiatrists, certified clinical psychologists, and licensed counseling psychologists, the clinical social worker is among the group of professionals who may legally provide psychotherapy to the members of the community through a private practice. However, licensed or certified clinical social workers are frequently members of a treatment team in community mental health centers, inpatient and outpatient hospital programs, drug and alcohol programs, rehabilitation agencies, and/or corrections facilities. They may have specialities in individual, group, family, or child therapy. Some clinical social workers act as consultants to schools and other agencies. Occasionally schools hire clinical social workers as part of their staffs to provide direct services to students and their families. These might include visits to the home for the special education home assessment, therapy for students, or facilitation during a parent/teacher conference.

Youth Services Worker: A youth services worker is a social worker who works for a state department of youth services. This department (which is referred to by different names in different states) is responsible for providing detainment and treatment of minors who have committed major crimes and who have been found to be "delinquent" by the court. The department of youth services staff does many of the same things a social worker does (see description of social worker) once the judge has found a juvenile guilty of a crime. They manage and supervise the student's rehabilitation program, which may include incarceration in a maximum security youth detention center or a supervised placement in the community. Some programs place juveniles in secure therapeutic treatment centers where they attend school and do strenuous and challenging physical activities. Other programs require students to do community service projects in their towns, such as cleaning up parks or helping the local highway department with road maintenance. The nature of the youth services treatment plan varies dramatically according to the severity of the crime and each state's resource for providing rehabilitative services. While some states incarcerate juveniles in detention centers, others find innovative ways to help students develop appropriate coping devices for a safe and productive return to the community.

Teachers may suggest that parents play an active role in the planning of a rehabilitation process. Progressive states are orienting their programs towards mainstreaming youthful offenders back into the community fairly rapidly. A major asset is the active participation of the parent and school in the student's program.

The more serious the student's adjustment problem, the more school and agency people are likely to be involved. It is important to know what their roles are and to be able to help parents to understand and use their resources. It is equally important to be familiar with the support services most schools offer through their regular education departments. Chapter Twelve describes many of these services.

10

Adding Regular Education Support Services

Chapter Ten deals with the development of a more comprehensive team of adults to help the student. If problems have persisted after you have tried and been unable to help, it is time to mobilize the special support services available in most schools. These support services provide you with a variety of resources. They should be strongly considered if the student is not adjusting to school. Chapter Ten begins with an overview of the various regular education support services that are available to you to use with students who have problems. It continues with a series of steps to be used for dealing with increasingly difficult school adjustment problems. Each step in the hierarchy of treatment options should be thought of as diagnostic. In other words, each step is a means to gather more information in preparation for a new plan if the previous one proves to be inadequate. The chapter concludes with a discussion of some of the advantages and pitfalls associated with building and working with a comprehensive team of parents, teachers, and support services personnel.

UNDERSTANDING REGULAR EDUCATION
SUPPORT SERVICES

Schools divide their educational programs and support services into two categories: *regular* and *special* education. Regular education programs are offered to all students in the district and constitute what we normally think of as the curricular and extracurricular activities. Special education services are offered to students who have special educational needs and have not learned up to their potential in regular education classes. Before these services can be provided, the school must do an *evaluation* to document a need for these "special services." Chapter Eleven presents a detailed discussion of "special services." However, there are many regular education support services for students. These may consist of the following, depending on your particular school:

- Guidance counseling
- Remedial educational support: remedial reading and writing classes, Chapter I tutoring
- Vocational counseling and placement services
- School nurse and health services
- Psychological services from the school psychologist
- Disciplinary support: from school principal or dean of students
- Extracurricular activities: athletics, clubs, music, and dramatic groups.

Some schools publish a student handbook and/or a pupil services handbook. These publications describe the services that are offered and explain the school's rules and policies. Copies of these documents can usually be found in the guidance or principal's office.

The support services offered may vary considerably from one school to another, so it is important for you to survey the resources that are available. This process involves finding out who else is available to join the team to help the student. A good first step is to consult the guidance office, which has an overview of the services that are available.

If you have attempted to help the student by using the steps outlined in the previous chapters and the student *continues* to have a problem or a crisis situation exists, it is time to seek additional resources. Any of the following situations would justify your consulting members of guidance counseling team.

- The student is having a hard time completing work.
- The student cannot attend school regularly.
- The student appears agitated or moody on a regular basis.
- The student reports conflicts with teachers and peers that never seem to be resolved.
- The student presents a serious management problem either at home or in school.
- The student talks about or is hurting herself or others.

THE GUIDANCE COUNSELOR/TEACHER TEAM

Consult the guidance counselor, who should be thought of as a "broker of information." She can help you decide on what step to take next. If the counselor feels a crisis situation exists, she may mobilize additional special resources very rapidly. At such times the principal, school nurse/pediatrician, and/or school psychologist may be consulted.

However, more commonly, the guidance counselor will request a conference between the parent and additional teachers who work with the student. The counselor should request information from each of the teachers who is working with the student.

Use the guidance counselor as a "case manager" and primary gatherer of information. She is in the best position to collect information and direct you to additional regular or special education supportive services. Discuss what alternatives the guidance counselor sees. Use the following guidelines to help choose your next step:

FINDING HELP FOR SPECIFIC PROBLEMS

Academic If the student lacks basic reading, math, or writing skills, explore a change in class placement to a different level of instruction with more individual help. Consider after-school remedial help if it is offered. Explore placement in a Chapter I remedial program. If these fail, discuss the possibility of a referral for special education screening.

Emotional If the student seems to be upset, confused, or unhappy, explore the possibility of supportive counseling with the guidance counselor. Request a conference with the school psychologist. The psychologist may conduct an evaluation and then suggest one of the following:

- Counseling
- Referral for additional services within the school
- Referral for therapy services at a community agency
- Referral for a special education evaluation

Attendance: If the student is not attending school more than 85 percent of the time and/or is falling behind in his classwork, contact the principal's or guidance office for advice and support. Evaluate the causes of the absenteeism and develop a plan to help the student attend school more often. If that fails, consider referring the student to the principal's office for an evaluation with one or more of the following:

- The school psychologist
- A local community mental health agency
- The probation officer at the local district court
- Special education staff
- An attendance officer

Behavior: If the student has a behavior management problem and cannot be controlled through a cooperative program between parent and classroom teacher, contact the principal's office and request that disciplinary procedures be used to help provide the student with additional structure.

If the student has already been involved with the school principal or assistant principal and the problem continues to exist, follow the steps listed to attain help from the support services staff or outside agencies. If there is still no change, make a referral to special education to determine whether or not the student is eligible for services.

HELPING PROBLEM STUDENTS PRIOR TO SPECIAL EDUCATION

If you have worked out a coordinated team approach and conditions still do not improve, then it makes sense to contact the regular education support specialists and build a more comprehensive team. At any time, one of those specialists might immediately refer the case to another service if he determines that a crisis exists, but in most cases an initial attempt is made to work with parents to treat the problem first. The entire time your team tries to help the student, whether or not things get better, you are gathering valuable information to be presented to additional people whom you may ask to join your team at a later date. So, your time is not wasted if the student does not improve through your initial efforts. There is a balance between the one extreme of using an oversimplified approach and the other extreme of calling together a large comprehensive team when one is not needed.

The following list of interventions can be used to assist you in the process of making the decision of what to do next. The list begins with relatively simple approaches to helping the student and builds to more complicated and time-consuming approaches. It both summarizes and builds on the management structures discussed in previous chapters. However, if at any time you feel that the student is in serious physical or emotional danger, a specialist should be consulted immediately.

STEP 1. Discuss the problem with the student.

- Point out that you are aware she is having a problem.
- Explain that you want to help her do better in school or at home.

- Ask the student what is needed from adults to improve her school performance.
- Help the student to understand a specific plan of action.
- Let the student know when and how you will monitor her progress.
- Explain to the student that it is very important for students to solve problems on their own if they can, but if it is too difficult to do, you will provide additional help: (i.e. step 2).
- Point out what you will do next if they can't fix things on their own.

STEP 2. Provide a regular after-school or home study period. Arrange a time for the student to do homework or make up work on a regular basis. The teacher might choose a study period or one day after school for the student to work under his supervision; with your encouragement a parent might arrange a regular time each evening for the student to do homework.

STEP 3. Develop a reward system to reinforce step 2. Find a positive reward that will be provided to the student if she is making progress toward solving the problem.

STEP 4. Increase the frequency of the information feedback system between the classroom and the home. Require the student to deliver a monitoring sheet to the teacher. Teachers can issue the sheet periodically for parents to monitor. The monitoring sheet must give specific details as to whether or not the student has achieved the target behavior.

Decide how often the student is to bring home information; increase the frequency from monthly to bimonthly to weekly or even daily reports according to the success the student has in improving his or her performance. Perhaps an information check-off sheet is needed only several times a year at a time when the student has not completed an assignment. Require information any time it is necessary to assure the student's success in completing tasks. (Younger students should be prompted by the teacher to take a monitoring sheet home; older students can be given the responsibility of reminding their instructor to initial the sheet.) If the management system you have developed is effective, the student can and should be given this responsibility.

STEP 5. Increase the strength of your management structure by restricting the student's privileges. By this time in the series of steps you have taken, you may have required the student to study at night on a regular basis, seek out an instructor after school once or twice a week, or bring home daily information to the parent. You may have reinforced the whole structure with rewards and disciplinary consequences. Throughout this entire series of steps, the primary responsibility for change is on the student, and the adults have played the role of managers. Students who do not have serious adjustment problems will generally respond well to this system of structuring their time and delivering information home about their performances. Many students do better when they are confident that they have a means to help the adults around them to be informed about school progress. The collecting and passing of information from teacher to parent on a regular basis introduces an element of accountability and responsibility that most students appreciate and to which they respond well.

If the student continues to struggle with schoolwork or to have adjustment problems in the home or community, additional services should be sought. But you, with the help of the parent, have made a good start. Working together with a large number of other adults can sometimes be frustrating and complicated. The next section provides some guidelines for working on such a team.

BUILDING A LARGER TEAM

A team offers a high potential for problem resolution because of the rich array of resources that are available, but it also can become cumbersome and potentially make it more difficult to help the student.

The first step in constructing an effective team approach is to identify the adults who have some potential to help the students with the identified problem. Including either too many or too few team players can lead to problems. Important adults who are excluded can either intentionally or inadvertently undermine the team's effort to provide appropriate intervention for the student. But the team should be kept as small as possible by including only those adults who are crucial to the process of carrying out the desired program. The more people involved, the more difficult it is to schedule meetings, keep everyone informed, resolve differences, and ultimately come to consensus about difficult decisions.

Next, define the problem in clear behavioral terms. A good definition of the problem will help you to focus on specific behaviors and decide who should be included on the team.

Finally, identify the parent(s), school staff, and/or outside agency personnel who (1) can provide information about the nature of the problem; (2) have expertise in locating treatment resources; (3) can gather ongoing information for the purpose of monitoring; (4) can design a specific treatment plan; (5) will carry out a treatment plan; and (6) will provide consequences, rewards, or restrictions for the student in response to the treatment.

Excuse adults who can provide initial information to help the process begin but are not needed to directly support the treatment process once it is underway. Clarify the role of each member of the team. Discuss the particular task each member will perform and determine if other resources are needed or if redundancies exist.

For example, one person should be designated as the clearing house for information. In a team consisting of two parents, a guidance counselor, a principal, and five teachers, the guidance counselor might be given the role of the person whom the parents call for biweekly reports from teachers. This simplifies the role of the parents by eliminating the need for them to call all five individual teachers. Likewise, by providing the guidance counselor information on a regular basis, teachers are not burdened with having to make separate contact with parents.

By developing a team of school staff members and carrying out the intervention steps in this chapter, you have done what you could to help the student within the limitations of regular education resources. Even if the student's grades and behavior do not improve, you have accomplished a number of things. You have gathered valuable information and tried many different ways to help the student. The information about how the student has responded to your efforts generates additional information about the problem. All this information puts you in an excellent position to make a well-documented argument for additional services.

Special education administrators are required by both local school policy and state regulations to provide an evaluation to determine if a student's problem justifies the expenditure of additional school funds for special education services. You have also clearly and concretely communicated to the students that the important adults in their lives are aware of their problems, trying to help them solve the problem, and continuing to try to find some way to make things better.

Students who believe that you understand their problems and are trying to help them are at less risk than those who think no one has noticed their pain and frustration. Once students agitate the surrounding network of adults and sound an alarm, they will have the tendency to relax their drive to produce symptoms. Their school adjustment problems have served a purpose; their symptoms have mobilized help.

Helping school students is developmental; it is a step-by-step process with the success of each succeeding step dependent upon the previous one. Each step sets the stage for the next step, as it produces valuable information about what will or will not work. Each attempt a team makes to help a student can be compared to using filters or screens to sort out materials. Sometimes a student can be helped with one quick pass of a coarse screen. Even though there may be many large holes in this screen, it might be enough. Compare this to step 1, just talking to the student. If you can help the student to do better with a supportive "pep" talk, that is effective. Then, as you tighten up the screen so that there are smaller and smaller holes, you begin to diagnose the severity of the problem. At a certain point a percentage of school students will fall through the tightest screens and filter out into the category of students with "special needs." This brings us to the next chapter, concerning the treatment of students who qualify for services beyond those offered by most school's regular education offerings: special education.

Part IV

SPECIAL EDUCATION

11

The Comprehensive Special Education Support Team

Federal law PL 94-142 states that each student between the ages of 3 and 21 has the right to a "free, appropriate public education." It makes each public school responsible to diagnose problems that interfere with students' learning and to provide an educational environment that offers them an opportunity to learn to their full potentials. It is the responsibility of each state and the local school committees to interpret and carry out this law. The way in which the law is interpreted and the language used to reinforce it vary from state to state. The task of educating all students, regardless of their disabilities or learning problems, is, therefore, a monumental task that is handled in many different ways by different school systems.

The team that works with the student with special needs is the primary advocate for that student. That role involves working with parents to join forces with the special education staff to construct an effective plan of action to begin to help students. It is not within the scope of this book to interpret the special education law in your state or to suggest any particular ways it should be carried out. The following section will, however, give you some tools for interpreting what your state's law requires.

The fundamental concern each parent and teacher has is whether or not the student is learning. If you have exhausted every resource within the domain of regular education services and the student continues to show delays in learning that are significantly greater than other students in the same age and ability group, then it is time to make a referral to special education.

It is your job to help start to build a case for special education. Teachers know the student better than the specialists do prior to referral to those specialists. You are the expert in several ways. If you have followed the steps in previous chapters, you have a clear idea of what the student can and cannot do in the classroom, and you know which approaches seem to work or seem to not work. This information is extremely valuable to all educational specialists. They depend on your information to begin to develop a plan to help the student. Guided by your valuable background information, specialists have a much better chance of being inducted into the team of adults who are building the case for special services. The goal of continued evaluation with the help of specialists is to demonstrate to the special education administrator that the student requires additional support. While it is the job of that administrator to coordinate all the services for both evaluation and treatment of special problems, she does not know the student until your team gathers and provides information. So, who are these "specialists" and which students qualify for "special education"?

UNDERSTANDING EDUCATIONAL AND PSYCHOLOGICAL RESOURCE SPECIALISTS

Specialists are staff members who have been trained in specific areas to diagnose and treat students with problems. They may be found on either special education or regular education staffs and may, in some cases, be administrators who have special skills and abilities. The regular and special education administrative offices will be able to help match you with the appropriate specialist. It is common in many schools to have an adjustment counselor or guidance counselor work with you to facilitate this process. Schools also have a referral procedure designed to orchestrate the process of evaluating a student for services. If you have already worked in a team with the regular education support services staff, the process of making a special education referral may be a natural extension of that team's effort.

There is potentially a wide range of special skills and abilities that school staff members may have. Your school system, depending on its size and the manner in which it interprets the special education law, may or may not have specialists in the following areas:

Psychological Assessment Specialists
Role: To assess the student's academic potential
       To diagnose intellectual strengths and weaknesses
       To screen for psychological adjustment
       problems and neurological problems

Educational Assessment Specialists
Role: To determine current levels of academic functioning; to screen for learning disabilities
       To determine learning styles

Family/Social Work Specialists
Role: To meet with parents to obtain a family history relative to the student's school adjustment problem; to guide parents in finding additional sources of help if needed
       To develop a parent/school team.

Medical Assessment Specialists
Role: To screen for medical problems that may affect the student's learning

Language, Speech, and Hearing Specialists
Role: To screen for problems in the areas of hearing, speaking, understanding language, and expressing ideas through language

Early Childhood Specialists
Role: To screen preschool students for entry into school programs; to make early diagnosis of any learning, emotional, or developmental problems; to provide instruction to students

Disciplinary Specialists
Role: To assess the student's behavioral performance and
        to provide disciplinary structure within school
        To support discipline in the classroom; to assist in
        making referrals to outside agencies if necessary

The following additional list of specialists may be available
on a part-time or "as needed" basis in some schools (their
roles have been described in Chapter Nine):

Pediatrician
Developmental pediatrician
Psychiatrist
Occupational therapist
Physical therapist
Family therapist
Neuropsychologist
Clinical psychologist
Social worker
Speech and language pathologist
School attendance officer

It may be possible to expand your team in some pretty
dramatic ways. There are potentially numerous resources to
mobilize. By consulting the school administration and guidance
staff, you can help to decide which resources to enlist. Most
specialists can also help you decide whether or not they may be of
service. With the support of your team and the approval of the
school administrator, you can now start to mobilize a more
comprehensive treatment team. Your role on that team will vary
according to the student's program and whether or not you are a
regular classroom teacher, special education teacher, or guidance
counselor.

QUALIFYING FOR SPECIAL EDUCATION SERVICES

There are two ways to address the issue of who qualifies for
special education, each representing a different point of view.
From the perspective of each local school system, students qualify

for special education if they meet the criteria set by their state and regional special education offices. School administrators are held accountable to their supervisory agencies and must therefore have ample documentation of special education need for any student whose education has required extra money.

From the point of view of the classroom teacher, the counselor, and the parent, help should be provided to any students who are not learning up to their potential. If help through regular education funds and resources fail, then why not seek special education?

Just how these two potentially divergent viewpoints are resolved presents a challenge to the parent/school team. Each local school committee has its own guidelines specifying which student with special needs it can legally serve; the burden of proof of these needs falls upon the parent, teacher, and evaluation specialists who must help to coordinate the efforts of all the adults who have worked with the student and present a case to determine eligibility. The decision, in some cases, becomes a question of interpretation. Consequently, the divergent points of view of team members provide a crucial element of checks and balances. In some cases, a disability may be very obvious, and the law is very clear about the local education association's responsibility. In others, it may be very difficult to judge eligibility. If this happens, the school and family may need to use the resources of the state department of education's arbitration or appeals process. (This is handled by each state's regional education office staff.) For example,

> A student who is mildly retarded and cannot hear well enough to be in a regular class has an obvious disability; all states should provide help. A student who fidgets, cannot concentrate, and makes careless errors may or may not have a disability that would make him or her eligible for special services.

So, ultimately, the question of which students are eligible for special services is a matter of interpretation of the law by each local educational association and its designated administrator of special education. However, your team's ability to advocate for the student in a competent and nonadversarial manner can make a significant difference. A list follows of the kinds of school problems that should qualify students for special education help:

> Limited mental ability.
>
> Physical disability: immobility, limited dexterity, vision deficit, hearing impairment, cerebral palsy, and so on.
>
> Emotional problems: anxiety, depression, fear, uncontrolled anger, impulsivity, (Chapter One presents eight sketches of students with social or emotional school adjustment problems.)
>
> Learning disabilities and attention problems: difficulty with processing, organizing, and expressing information; inability to attend to and focus on classwork.
>
> Behavior problems: inability to follow rules, learn from past experience, and demonstrate appropriate consideration for other people.

Frequently these categories overlap, and one problem may lead to another. It requires a team of parents, teachers, and special education staff to understand fully the nature and scope of a problem. You now have the tools to be an integral member of that team and to function as a competent advocate for the student. It would be presumptuous to describe how any particular school should treat any particular student. But you can continue your role as educational caretaker and advocate for the student by continuing to work with the special education team until a program has been established for the student.

DISCOVERING WHAT SPECIAL EDUCATION CAN DO

Students who are found to be eligible for special education services represent a group of students with a wide variety of problems. To help them overcome school problems and to function according to their academic abilities, schools potentially offer many different services. The local education association hires specialists to provide these services, which may include all of or any of the following:

Remedial Instruction

This is instruction for students who have been unable to learn to read, write, and do mathematics through the curriculum provided within the regular educational setting.

Tutorial Assistance

Tutorial assistance provides help for students in maintaining an adequate performance in their classes. It may involve helping students to understand and complete their assigned work and to make up missed work.

Structured Study Hall

Structured study halls provide students with supervision and support for using their time effectively. Students may be taught how to keep an assignment notebook and to budget their time effectively to complete their work on time. Tutorial assistance may be provided within the study hall setting.

Monitoring

Monitoring systems gather performance information on a regular basis and help to activate the use of other resources such as tutorial help or home-based support structures. If a student's performance indicates that the amount of special education services needs to be decreased or increased, the parent/school team will be alerted through a good monitoring system. Students who are monitored are taught to understand and use to advantage the teachers' reports on their classroom performance.

Case Management

Frequently, special education students have diverse or complicated educational plans. Case management services coordinate the efforts of all the adults who are involved with the student. If information needs to be gathered and shared with other team members or a crisis occurs, the case manager acts as a clearing house of information and initiates any modification to the program of special services.

Special Education Classroom Instruction

Special education programs offer an alternative course of studies that is calibrated to meet the specific learning needs of the students. These classes are smaller than regular classes and use different instructional materials. Academic tasks are frequently broken down into smaller units of instruction. Instructors can individualize work, present high interest curriculums, and provide extra help and support.

Learning Disabilities Instruction

This is for students who have a problem receiving, processing, and expressing information due to learning disabilities. Help can be provided in a variety of ways. Students can be taught special problem-solving strategies to be used in their regular classes. They may also be placed in a special education classroom for a specific course where the specialist can help them learn to compensate for their disability and provide close supervision of their learning process. Frequently, special learning devices are used to provide a variety of ways for students to solve problems. These include calculators and word processors, games and enrichment materials, and objects that can be manipulated to help students understand difficult concepts.

Language, Speech, and Hearing Services

These services help students in the areas of hearing, understanding, processing, and expressing language. Services ranges from helping deaf students to receive both oral and visual information to helping other students without a hearing disability to understand language better and to express their ideas more clearly.

Access for the Physically Disabled

The federal special education laws PL 94-142 and 504 are designed to provide access to educational facilities to all handicapped students. Schools have the responsibility to provide appropriate aides to students whose educational needs could be met in the public school building. They must have physical access to that building. In addition, special education services can provide additional devices or teaching assistants to help disabled students use the public school resources. (A publication of the Children's Defense Fund, "94-142 and 504: Numbers That Add Up to Educational Rights for Handicapped Children: A Guide for Parents and Advocates," by Yohalem and Dinsmore, 1978, outlines how federal law 504 specifies that schools must provide physical access to students with physical disabilities.)

Occupational Therapy

Some school students require specific and specialized therapy to help them with the physical manipulation of the environment around them. Occupational therapy can help them to develop better dexterity and muscle tone to enable them to participate in a greater number of physical activities.

Physical Therapy

Some students have limited physical mobility and require therapy to stretch, strengthen, and mobilize their bodies. If their educational development is hampered by this kind of disability, a special education plan may include physical therapy.

Vocational/Occupational Education and Counseling

One of the ultimate goals of special education is to assure that students are educated to their potentials and to help them be as self-sufficient and independent as possible. Occupational education is a crucial service most schools provide to help capitalize on many years of special intervention with students. These programs help to prepare secondary level students with skills and information that will facilitate their successful pursuit of employment or higher education.

Counseling or Therapy

Some students are unable to learn due to psychological problems. Counseling with trained school specialists or therapists from local community health agencies is sometimes the only way that a student with an emotional disability can be helped. Frequently, the therapeutic work with the student requires the participation of the parents to assure a consistent team approach.

Home Tutorials

Students who have an injury or long-term illness that prevents them from keeping up with their academic work qualify for special education services. The school can provide a professional tutor to give instruction in the home. In some cases, home tutoring may be provided to students who have psychological problems and/or who are waiting for placement in a day or residential program (see the discussion that follows).

Programs for Severely Handicapped Students

While the federal special education law charges each local education association with the role of providing each disabled student with reasonable access to the mainstream of regular education, some students have educational needs that cannot be properly met there. It would simply be harmful to force a student to stay in a setting where he or she cannot be successful. There are, therefore, school- and community-sponsored day programs that provide students with a special curriculum that is designed to meet their special needs and to help them be more successful learners. Special day programs deal with students with very limited intellectual abilities, moderate to severe emotional problems, and profound physical disabilities. Students who are blind or deaf may also be placed by some local education associations in a day program. If the problems are severe, the student may be placed in a residential facility. In residential programs students live on the campus or grounds and have an educational-therapeutic program available to them 24 hours a day.

Devices for Handicapped

Special education services may provide equipment, tools, or devices of many kinds to assist the student in gaining access to the resources they need in order to learn.

THE NEED FOR ADVOCACY

There are additional services some schools may be able to offer a student with special education needs; on the other hand, some of the services listed may not fall within the range of offerings in your state or local education associations. Therefore, it remains the responsibility of all the members of the team to investigate and recommend any service they believe might help the student. It is the role of the school administrators of each local education association and the personnel from the state departments of education to determine what services can be offered to the student. If you don't advocate for services, it is possible no one else will. Parents, teachers, and guidance counselors can initiate a referral to special education by filling out a referral form and submitting it to the appropriate administrator. The staff in the school principal's office and the office of the administrator of special education can help you obtain a referral form.

KNOWING WHAT TO EXPECT ONCE A SPECIAL EDUCATION REFERRAL IS MADE

As a team member, you now know how to try to help a student prior to a special education referral. You have a general sense of what kinds of specialists and services might be offered. This information places you in a better position to be an advocate and an effective team member. But the process of locating, evaluating, and treating special needs students is sometimes complicated and tedious. The next sections of this chapter will present you with a series of guidelines for what to expect during the various aspects of the special education process. First, there is an outline of what to expect about the team evaluation process from the time you identify and refer a student. Then, there is a description of what to look for when a specific service has been assigned. This will give you information about the various components of the special education process and services that are potentially provided.

There are many concerned adults on the team by now, so it is necessary to describe expectations from a number of different points of view. A well-coordinated, well-integrated team is characterized by a division of labor, with various team members playing uniquely different, but complementary roles. As with many tasks that have to be accomplished by a group of people, there is the potential for both cooperation and dissension. People develop strong opinions about what they believe is best for a student in need. Conflicts will arise. Having a list of reasonable expectations can help you be patient with the process, yet assertive if necessary.

Throughout the book you have seen the importance of looking at things from multiple points of view. The perspective of parents is presented here to help you anticipate what they may experience during the special education referral, evaluation, and treatment process. The more you can demonstrate to parents that you understand the difficulties of their situation, the more likely you can keep them as active and productive members of the team. Helping parents to know what to expect before the special education process begins can be effective in helping them to be realistic about the kinds of feelings and frustrations they may feel. Special education can seem like a burden to you as well. There are expectations school systems have for the regular education teacher that may be difficult to understand and to carry out. The next section of the chapter outlines what both parents and teachers can expect from special education.

(Note: Until this point in the text, the word "team" has referred to a group of adults who have joined together to coordinate an effort to help the student. The federal special education law PL 94-142 also uses the word "team" to refer to the group of people who are formally invited to or requested to participate in the process of defining the student's special education needs as the result of an evaluation. The process is called a "team evaluation." This formal team will henceforth be referred to by use of capitals: "TEAM.")

Administrative Review and Assessment

Once a special education referral is made, an administrator reviews the referral document and forwards it to the special education administrator's office. The special education administrator also reviews the referral and requests written permission from the parent (or student if 18 years old or older) to begin a formal evaluation process. Then the special education administrator selects appropriate assessments to be performed. These *usually* include assessments of the following:

- Educational history
- Current school status: academic and disciplinary
- Intellectual ability and psychological status
- Family and developmental history
- Past and present medical concerns

Assessment *may also* include the following:

- A language, speech, and hearing assessment
- A special education specialist's assessment
- A psychiatric assessment
- A neurological assessment
- An English as a second language assessment
- Any additional specialist's assessments deemed appropriate by the special education administration or requested by a parent

Establishment of a Meeting Date

Within 30 days a date is set for a meeting of the parent(s) and all appropriate school staff members and specialists. Parents should be invited to review the student's records and consult any specialists or advocates before they attend the meeting if they would like to.

An IEP Is Developed

A meeting is held to develop an Individualized Educational Plan or IEP. During the IEP TEAM meeting, assessments are presented and discussed. A statement of the student's special education needs is developed, and after the meeting a liaison is assigned. It is the role of the special education liaison to coordinate the writing of the individualized education plan and to present this plan to the administrator of special education for approval. The IEP must be prepared within ten days.

Services Are Designated

The IEP is reviewed by the administrator of special education, and an appropriate special education service is designated. The IEP is presented to the parent for review, approval, and signature. If the parent wishes to modify the IEP, he discusses his proposed changes with the liaison and/or special education administrator. Changes can be made with the approval of the special education administrator. The IEP liaison reviews the IEP with all other members of the team of adults who are concerned with helping the student. The special education service is provided to the student.

What to Tell the Parent to Expect During the IEP Process

You can assume that any parent who has a student who is struggling with school or has any other adjustment problem is a worried parent. No one likes to worry, particularly about problems that do not seem to be getting any better. It is important that you communicate to parents that you realize how difficult it must be to cope with this situation. It is hard for parents to share the problem with unfamiliar people. It may be relatively easy for them to discuss the problem with the family doctor or a friend, but when subjected to a comprehensive team evaluation process, they may feel as if they are being placed under a huge microscope. Predictably, that can be a very uncomfortable feeling.

TEAM evaluations can involve more than a dozen people, all trying to help, but at the same time all responsible for probing the school, student, and family to understand the true nature of the problem. This necessary scrutiny is not enjoyable for you or the parent. It is wise to help parents realize that the TEAM evaluation process, no matter how sensitively and expertly carried out, may seem intrusive and difficult to understand. By doing this you help to prevent them from becoming confused, disillusioned, and resistant.

Some parents may already have strong relationships with other members of the parent/school team and feel a sense of trust and mutual respect for the school staff. That is the best way to go into the special education evaluation process. Other parents may have had frustrating experiences with the school. They may not have developed a sense of trust and cooperation with anyone on the staff. So the first thing to expect when the process begins is for them to feel somewhat vulnerable and manipulated. If you anticipate this reaction, you can attempt to make the process as nonthreatening and supportive as possible.

The more information parents have about the process, the less likely they are to become uncooperative. You can say to them that

- They should expect the school to secure their permission to initiate the TEAM evaluation process and to invite them to attend the meeting. That they have the right to know why the school is concerned about their child and should schedule a meeting with the appropriate staff member and find out what she thinks the problem is.
- If they do not agree with the school, they are not required by law to grant you their consent for the TEAM process. Point out that they must realize two important things:
  - If the school thinks the student needs extra help, there is probably a good reason.

- Just because they give consent to the evaluation does not mean they have agreed to particular services or a course of action. They should think of the evaluation as gathering information, which can make them better informed decision makers. Schools must attain their consent to deliver services to their child, so they have not agreed to anything until they have signed an individual educational plan.

● They can request that a special education administrator be available to them before the TEAM meeting to answer any questions they may have concerning the following:
    - The regulations in your state regarding students with special education needs
    - Their rights as parents
    - The specific time line and nature of the process on which they are about to embark
    - What to do if they disagree with the school or do not want a certain assessment performed

● They should be able to understand the assessments and may request a written copy of an assessment if they wish, and if they have questions or concerns, they should expect to be able to meet with the specialist who wrote the assessment to allow her to discuss and interpret her findings. However, you must not recommend that they attempt to interpret specialists' written assessments without the professional guidance of a staff member.

● They should participate actively in a process of competent decision making based on thorough research and careful processing of all available information.

● They should expect to be presented with a written individual educational plan within about two school weeks.

● They will be expected to review, sign, and return the individual educational plan to your special education administrator. If they do not understand any aspect of the IEP or do not agree with the plan, they do not have to sign it. Explain that the special education liaison assigned to them should be available to discuss the IEP with them.

How to Describe an Educational Plan to Parents

As the parents become involved in the IEP process, they need to know what the various components of the educational plan mean. Typically a special education staff member explains the plan to parents. Occasionally the regular classroom teacher has this role. Regardless of which role you may have adopted, here is a list of elements of a sample educational plan, with a description of each part.

1. *Profile* describing the student's current school situation, learning style, strengths and weaknesses, and the way in which he or she takes in, processes, and expresses information. It should serve as a brief overview of the student's special education needs.
2. *List of modifications* to the school policy concerning
   a. Classroom procedures.
   b. Adaptations to physical education.
   c. Modifications of the disciplinary code.
   d. The awarding of credit and graduation requirements.
   e. Participation in state-mandated basic skills testing programs.
   f. Transportation.
   g. Support service to regular education teachers.
   h. The cost of services.
3. *Identification and description of service*
   a. When, where, and how often a special service is to be provided.
   b. The person who will provide the service.

     c. The size and description of the instructional setting.

     d. When the service should begin.

     e. At what point in the student's development the service should end.

4. Set of *goals and objectives* to direct the instructional staff toward teaching the student and evaluating his or her progress.

     a. A description of *teaching methodology* and an instructional approach for each goal.

     b. A description of a *method to evaluate* progress and monitor the student.

     c. Each general goal should be followed by several *specific objectives*. These objectives should state the desired outcomes of the special education program.

How to Evaluate an Educational Plan

An educational plan is a contract. A contract must contain a clear explanation of all the elements of the agreement between the school and the family. It should present an outline of the anticipated outcomes of that agreement. You can evaluate an educational plan by determining whether or not it answers the following questions:

1. Is every aspect of the agreement between the school and the family described clearly?

2. Are the specific objectives written in clear and descriptive behavioral terms, that is, Do they ask the student to do things that adults can directly observe?

3. If you could unobtrusively watch the student perform these new behaviors in the classroom, would you be convinced that he has made a significant improvement in his school performance?

If you cannot answer "yes" to all three questions, you may need to request that the team continue to revise this special contract. Evaluating the content of the child's educational plan is a valuable process because it forces all the adults on the team to identify and resolve differences before the treatment phase of the program begins. If differences are resolved in the context of reasonable negotiation, future conflict situations may be averted as a result.

The sample educational plan form presented here is a document that contains all the elements of a complete contract between the school and the parent. The completed sample educational plan that follows it provides an example of a form after it has been completed. After reading the example, ask yourself the three questions posed earlier. Use this method to practice evaluating the quality of educational plans.

SAMPLE EDUCATION PLAN FORM
(based on educational plan form used by
the Commonwealth of Massachusetts)

----

1.   STUDENT INFORMATION:

Type of Meeting (annual review, initial evaluation, or three-year reevaluation)

Name: Date of meeting:
Grade: Dates plan covers:
Birth date:
Age:
School:
Dominant language:
Address:
Parents' names:
Home phone:
Work phone:

Meeting participants:

Signature of participants:

------------------   ------------------   ------------------

------------------   ------------------   ------------------

2.   STUDENT PROFILE:

3.   ADDITIONAL INFORMATION:

4.   DESCRIPTION OF SERVICE:

5.   TRANSPORTATION PLAN:

6.   GENERAL GOALS:

GOAL 1

Current Level of Performance:

Teaching Approach:

Method of Monitoring and Evaluating:

Student-Centered Specific Objective:

GOAL 2

Current Level of Performance:

Teaching Approach:

Method of Monitoring and Evaluating:

Specific Student-Centered Objectives:

GOAL 3

Current Level of Performance:

Teaching Approach:

Method of Monitoring and Evaluating:

Specific Student-Centered Objectives:

ETC.

SAMPLE EDUCATION PLAN (completed)

1.   STUDENT INFORMATION:

Type of Meeting: ANNUAL REVIEW

Name: Al Duit   Date of meeting: 12/15/87
Grade: 7   Dates plan covers: 1/87 to 1/88
Birth date: 1974
Age: 12
School: -------
Dominant language: ENGLISH
Address: 10 MAIN STREET
Parents' names: MR. AND MRS. DUIT
Home phone: 111-1111
Work phone: 222-2222

Meeting Participants: ---------------------------

Signature of Participants:

-----------------   -----------------   -----------------

-----------------   -----------------   -----------------

2. STUDENT PROFILE

Al is a friendly, impulsive seventh grade boy who has underachieved in most subjects in school. His writing skills are about two years below grade level, and he makes many careless errors in mathematics. When his instructors spend extra time with him, his performance improves briefly. Al continually confuses details and cannot follow directions. He needs information presented to him both visually and orally. Tutoring by teachers after school and special attention in his regular classes have not helped him improve his school performance.

3. ADDITIONAL INFORMATION

Al can take regular physical education classes and does not require a modification of the school disciplinary code. His participation in mandatory basic skills testing should be modified. Basic skills tests should be administered to Al in a setting isolated from other students, and the tests should be untimed.

4. DESCRIPTION OF SERVICE
Special Education Remedial Writing Program: 1 period per day.
Special Education Monitoring: 1 period per day.

5. TRANSPORTATION PLAN: Al will ride the regular bus to school.

6. GENERAL GOALS

GENERAL GOAL 1: TO IMPROVE BASIC SKILLS IN WRITING

Current Level of Performance
Al has basic skills deficits in writing and language arts; it appears that his poor performance is related to poor organizational skill and impulsivity. He functions on the fifth grade level in writing.

Teaching Approach
Tutoring and remedial support, small highly structured, individualized instructional sessions; high interest materials and activities; programmed self-instruction materials; individualized, behavior management strategies.

Method of Monitoring and Evaluating
Observe and record on task and percentage of correct answers for Al's classes each day; send home progress reports to parents weekly; pre- and posttesting of writing skills.

Specific Student-Centered Objectives
1. Al will write paragraphs with topic sentences.
2. Al will demonstrate an organizational theme for each paragraph he writes.
3. Al will recognize and correct incomplete and run-on sentences.
4. Al will recognize and correct grammatical errors.
5. Al will produce revised copies of his first draft.

GOAL 2: TO IMPROVE ORGANIZATION, STUDY HABITS, AND SELF CORRECTING SKILLS

Current Level of Performance
Al is disorganized and impulsive in preparing most

Continued

163

classroom and homework assignments. His math performance is about two years below grade level, and he is failing his arithmetic course. Although he appears to understand concepts, he cannot follow directions or recognize when he makes mistakes.

Teaching Methodology and Approach
Al should be observed in his classes by a special education teacher; both special and regular education staff must collaborate on a strategy to structure his classroom experience so he self-corrects classwork and writes down his assignments. Information should be sent home to his parents on a weekly basis.

Method of Monitoring and Evaluating
Once a week Al should be rated on the percentage of careless errors he has located and corrected. A graph of his progress should be made and shared with both Al and his classroom teachers. Grade level equivalency testing in math should be done twice a year, in January and June.

Specific Student-Centered Objectives
1. Al will compute problems using basic math facts (addition, subtraction, multiplication, and division) with 85 percent accuracy.
2. Al will complete math problems with decimals and fractions with 80 percent accuracy.
3. Al will earn at least a "C" grade (70 percent in his basic seventh grade "Fundamentals of Arithmetic" course.
4. Al will learn and use organizing techniques such as preplanning, keeping an assignment book, and goal setting.
5. Al will follow directions the first time they are given.
6. Al will plan ahead of time (with teacher support) to gather materials and study for tests.
7. Al will begin to work on classroom assignments as soon as the instructor finishes explaining the directions.
8. Al will complete an assigned task before seeking adult feedback.
9. Al will accurately prepare and turn in all homework assignments on time.
10. Al will complete academic tasks within prescribed time limits.

Discussion Al's educational plan was written with these specific objectives because he could not perform them before his program began. Imagine that you could watch Al in his classroom through a one-way mirror. Would you have a specific idea of what behaviors to look for to determine if he is making progress in school? If Al could consistently demonstrate an ability to do a majority of the behaviors outlined in the "Specific Objectives" part of the educational plan, would you be convinced that his program is meeting his special education needs? Use these questions to decide if an educational plan is written clearly and outlines a program that you believe will help the child.

What Teachers Should Expect During the IEP Process

The first thing you can expect is to feel somewhat uncomfortable when a large group of people suddenly want to know why the student you have been trying to teach is not learning in your classroom. But as a member of the comprehensive team that has been trying to help the student prior to referral to special education, you already know that there are limitations to what you can do in your classroom. Your information is crucial to the TEAM evaluation process, and you can expect that process to involve you in the following ways:

- A specialist may come to observe a student in your classroom. Their observations will help you to describe the student of the IEP meeting.
- Members of the assessment team will ask you for your description of the student's behavior and classroom performance. The more concrete and noninterpretive you are, the more likely the TEAM can use your information effectively. You can participate in the process of making conclusions at the end of the TEAM Meeting once all the other reporters have given their information. Your statements should follow these guidelines:
  - Give specific descriptions of observable behaviors.

- Avoid stating what service the student should or should not have.
- Say what the student can and cannot do in your classroom.
- State the limitations of your current resources.

● Expect to be invited to the TEAM meeting to present your summary of information.

● Expect the special education staff member who has been designated liaison *to contact you* to explain your part in executing the IEP that has been developed.

● Expect to feel challenged and/or somewhat pressured to work with a student in a slightly different way than you normally do. The national trend in education is to return as many special education students as possible to the regular classroom. Sooner or later you will feel a pressure to expand your repertoire of skills and techniques to work with these students.

● Do expect technical assistance to carry out this task. This assistance may include any of the following:
- Training and workshops to help you become familiar with procedures and techniques you will be asked to use.
- Additional equipment, materials, and other special resources.
- Support personnel to assist you by providing direct or indirect help in your classroom if necessary.
- Active supervision by specialists and administrators; assurance that you are carrying out this special aspect of your job as competently as possible.

● Do not wait to ask for supervision until you feel a major problem exists or you have lost your confidence or patience; get help fast as a preventive measure. Keep your supervisor aware of how realistic it is to meet the student's special needs while you have 20 to 30 other students to teach at the same time. Think of everything you do as diagnostic; it provides additional information on how the student is functioning. If the student's placement in your classroom is still not working out, ask the special education liaison for guidance.

12

What to Look for in Special Education Programs

By the time a student is referred to special education, the team of adults trying to help the student is large. You play a crucial role on a complicated and diverse team. In previous parts of this book you have learned a variety of things you can do to try to help the student with a school adjustment problem.

With the introduction of special education, a great array of additional services and treatments is possible. Chapter Twelve familiarizes you with the various aspects of a special education program that may be found in your school. Of course, few schools have all the components listed. But you can acquire a specific idea of how the special services differ from your classroom and explore ways to coordinate and complement their approach to the student. If you perceive gaps in your special education delivery model, use the following list as a framework for designing and building the programs you think your school needs.

COMPREHENSIVE PROGRAM DESCRIPTION

A program description is a written document that presents a brief overview of the program and of the characteristics of the students it serves. The description is disseminated to the school staff and parents. It informs them about the program and describes the kinds of students who would be appropriately referred. It also describes the kind of services being offered and the criteria for students entering and leaving the program.

PROGRAM OBJECTIVES

Program objectives are a written set of general goals and specific objectives based on the needs of the target population of special students being served. The objectives are developed from interviews and surveys with parents, regular and special education teachers, guidance personnel, and administrators. Each specific program objective should describe an observable behavior that is an outcome or result of the program. Program objectives give all the members on the team a focus for reviewing and evaluating that program. They can be thought of as a counterpart of the IEP for the student and they serve as an excellent self-evaluation component for a program.

CURRICULUM

Each special education program will need to provide students with a modification of the traditional school course of studies. These modifications may vary from teaching identical materials in a different way to presenting the student with entirely different subject matter. The teaching approaches and special materials and equipment used in each program make up the curriculum. In some cases the curriculum will be individualized and stress basic skills, life skills, and/or high-interest activities.

DISCIPLINARY STRUCTURE

Each program needs a set of procedures providing consequences for disruptive and/or uncooperative behavior of students. Any difference from the procedures published in the student handbook for regular education students should be clearly defined and pointed out to both student and parent. This is the primary structure for making disciplinary decisions, including whether a student should leave the program and be referred to a different setting.

BEHAVIOR MANAGEMENT

A behavior management program is a set of procedures by which staff provide both positive and negative consequences as a way of altering student behavior. A program should make use of positive rewards whenever possible to help motivate students who have found difficulty deriving intrinsic rewards from school. In addition, a set of negative consequences should be available to increase the strength of the management program at times when the curriculum, behavior management procedures, and disciplinary procedures are not effective in helping students to control their behaviors.

MONITORING SYSTEM

Students, staff, and parents all need to know what progress is being made during the special education program. A monitoring system should provide a regular flow of information to accomplish the following:

1. Assist the staff in making program decisions.
2. Help students to become aware of their performance.
3. Provide parents with the information they need to set up home-based supports.
4. Give administrators information on the status of the program so they can help supervise, troubleshoot problems, and be supportive to staff. The information collected might represent any or all of the following categories:
   a. The percentage of time the student is absent or tardy.
   b. The amount of homework being completed on a daily or weekly basis.

  c. The number of missed, inadequate, or incomplete classroom assignments for each week.

  d. The amount of time the student spends in detention or a time-out room each week.

  e. The percentage of time the student is observed by the teacher to be on task (i.e., making an obvious effort to complete the work placed before him).

  f. The grades earned on assignments, tests, quizzes, homework, and so on.

  g. The number of times each week the student has a crisis or has to report to the school nurse.

Each special education program should describe what areas it monitors, how often, and to whom information is reported. Depending on the type of student with whom a program works, information could be sent home with the student, mailed home, or phoned home. The frequency of reporting can range from daily to monthly, but it should be done on a regular basis and not be restricted to those times when a serious crisis occurs.

TEAMWORK WITH PARENTS

No special education program can operate to its fullest potential without either the active or passive consent of the parent. Some parents are not in the position to play an active role due to restrictions on their time; others are able to be available to special education staff for phone conferences or meetings. Each program should outline the various roles parents can play to help support the educational process.

COUNSELING

Most special education students require some kind of counseling. This may range from supportive or directive counseling to help students with specific minor problems to intensive therapy. Programs that work with students who have serious psychological problems need to have staff members who have formal training in counseling, including a clinically supervised practical internship. These teachers must have skill in individual, group, and crisis counseling approaches. In some cases counseling is done by the staff spontaneously during the events of the day. In other cases students can be scheduled for regular meetings. When serious psychological problems prevent the school staff from helping the student, a referral to a professional psychotherapist or family therapist may be appropriate.

MAINSTREAMING

Mainstreaming is the practice of integrating special education students into regular classes. This process may involve phasing them back gradually after they have been in special classes and providing them with supportive services in those classrooms. As a student demonstrates that she can fulfill the objectives outlined on the Individualized Education Plan, it is crucial to provide her access to the mainstream of public school life. This should begin when the student learns to cope with the academic, social, and emotional stresses of school. When the student is mainstreamed, the amount of time she spends in the regular classroom should be increased gradually. Each step in the phasing process must be carefully monitored to assure the team that the student is making an adequate adjustment.

For programs designed to work with students who have serious emotional and behavior adjustment problems, these additional program components are necessary:

CLINICAL SUPERVISION

Each program should be supervised by a certified psychologist, psychiatrist, or licensed clinical social worker. Weekly supervision helps staff develop and modify therapeutic approaches to students who have emotional problems. The consultant may act as a liaison with any outside therapists and assist in the process of determining which students should enter or leave a program.

COURT LIAISON

For students who have problems attending school or who have broken the law, a relationship with the local district court is important. If presented with regular information on school performance, the probation officer can provide the student with an additional source of supervision and structure. He also can be instrumental in helping students and families find services from local community mental health agencies or treatment programs.

Not all schools will have all the program components I have just listed. You must advocate for including as many of them as you can in your schools. Students with special educational needs, particularly social and emotional needs, are grossly underserved. This happens because historically they have not been eligible for special education. Therefore, few programs exist that educators can use as models. Use the components discussed in Chapter Twelve to develop your own comprehensive programs.

Part V

SPECIAL TOPICS

13

Drug and Alcohol Abuse

WHAT IS SUBSTANCE ABUSE?

Substance abuse can be defined as the ingestion of either drugs or alcohol for the purpose of achieving an artificially pleasant emotional state that would otherwise not be available to a person. It involves the use of substances that are illegal or that violate school policy. Students who use drugs or alcohol in school are abusing these substances.

Drug and alcohol abuse become school adjustment problems when they interfere with the students' ability to function in school. This may be caused by students being caught and disciplined by school officials. In this case, they may miss school due to mandatory disciplinary action. Of more serious concern is substance abuse that impairs a student's ability to function both intellectually and psychologically. The degree to which students are impaired and/or miss school due to suspension determines how serious their substance abuse problem is. Estimations of how widespread this abuse is vary from researcher to researcher, but the consensus is that the problem is monumental. Between 50 and 60 percent of seventh graders report they have experimented with alcohol. When high school seniors were interviewed, the percentage of users rose to approximately 90 percent.[1]

Drugs and alcohol are used by students to produce altered emotional states. Their motivation varies from substance use to impress peers to use that helps alleviate their fear of failure or anxiety. Others are bored with school and lack motivation to become involved in more appropriate activities.[2,3] Rarely do students become drug or alcohol involved without some other adjustment problem serving as a catalyst. When school personnel detect a problem, students have already taken some risks by exposing themselves to teachers or administrators who must take strict disciplinary action. It is unusual for students to take a risk without some conscious or unconscious desire to relieve stress in their school and family lives. An exception is found in the case when a student's addiction is so strong that the risk becomes inconsequential.

Dependence on drugs and alcohol occurs in the absence of healthy psychological coping devices to resolve uncomfortable feelings and stresses. Fear of failure, anxiety about peer relationships, impatience, and hyperactivity each represents some of the many emotional states students seek to escape through substance abuse. Drug and alcohol abuse are often symptoms of other psychological and social problems experienced by school children. Heuer states that "Many times an addiction results as an approach to solving difficult life problems. Individuals who are searching for mechanisms to cope with perceived unmanageable issues turn to alcohol and other drugs as a solution and may eventually incorporate this problem-solving technique into their daily lifestyle."[4]

CHARACTERISTICS OF STUDENTS AT RISK FOR SUBSTANCE ABUSE

Students from families who abuse drugs and alcohol will have a tendency to also use drugs and alcohol. The modeling provided in the family contributes to this tendency in both obvious and subtle ways. Parents who use drugs set an example in the family that implies that use is acceptable. Even though parents may lecture their children about the dangers of drug use, the example they set provides the student with the message that under the right conditions, use may be permissible. A more significant contributing factor to drug abuse concerns the pattern of dealing with stressful situations that the family models. Children who grow up in families that do not demonstrate healthy and effective devices for resolving conflicts and dealing with stressful situations are robbed of a valuable learning experience. By not participating in a family system that consistently and actively teaches children how to face and resolve problems, these students never learn to build healthy coping devices. As a result, when they encounter problems in school or the community (as well as in their families), they do not possess the psychological tools to reduce stress. Consequently, they are at risk for substance abuse.

Although family patterns of dealing with stress influence many students who abuse substances, other factors related to school may add to the pressures they experience. Students who have problems adjusting to school are frequently underachievers. They cannot derive the rewards that most other students acquire from being successful in school. Failure in school undermines self-esteem and makes students more vulnerable to the artificial rewards of drugs and alcohol.

Students with attentional deficit hyperactivity disorder (ADHD) are particularly prone to substance abuse as they become older if they are not treated. Attentional deficit hyperactivity disorder is a syndrome characterized by hyperactivity, impulsivity, and distractibility. Refer to Chapter Fifteen for a list of characteristics typical of students with ADHD. ADHD is caused by an imbalance of the chemicals in the brain that are responsible for transmitting information. Although students can have ADHD with or without hyperactivity, their ability to remain focused on the classroom activities and to be patient during the completion of tedious tasks is severely impaired. It is believed that many students who have become substance abusers and/or youthful offenders may suffer from ADHD, although this hypothesis presents some controversy.

So who is at greatest risk for substance abuse in school? Students of parents who are abusers and students who perform poorly in school and may have problems controlling their impulses in the classroom. Does this mean that all substance abusers have this background? No. Peer pressures or other kinds of psychological problems also contribute to students turning to drugs. Some of the types of students presented in the behavioral sketches in Chapter One also represent students who may become dependent on drugs and/or alcohol to deal with their anxiety and stress.

HOW TO RECOGNIZE SUBSTANCE ABUSERS IN SCHOOL

Drug or alcohol involved students show their symptoms in both obvious and not so obvious ways. Severe abusers come to school under the influence and show erratic behavior. They may appear to be unable to focus on their work, answer questions in bizarre ways, not be in control of their body movements, and/or smell of alcohol. Students who use hallucinogenic drugs may experience psychotic behavioral episodes during which they appear to have a very limited capacity to show appropriate responses to the environment around them. These students may distort interactions with other students and teachers, seem overly sensitive to criticism, or be lethargic and unresponsive. In extreme cases a drug-or alcohol-involved student will become ill or pass out and require immediate medical attention. The following checklist created by Heuer (© 1985 M.A.C. Printing and Publishing Division; used by permission) serves as an excellent guide for teachers and counselors.

Physical symptoms include

Sleeplessness
Deterioration in physical care
Impaired ability to react to social cues
Frequent illness and shaking of the hands

Emotional symptoms include

Oversensitivity
Changes in areas of interest and social relationship
Secretiveness
Withdrawal
Moodiness
Apathetic attitude[5]

You will encounter students who have substance abuse problems but who do not display their symptoms in obvious ways. These students may have a dependency on drugs or alcohol, but are in enough control of their behavior at the time to hide the overt signs of the problem. The only way to detect substance abusers at this level is to examine their overall school performance and determine their general level of adjustment to school. The screening and assessment methods presented in Part One of this book serve as a step-by-step guide to this process. If students appear to have an impairment in their level of functioning, alcohol and drug abuse must be considered along with all the other potential adjustment problems students may have.

One consistent clue I have found with substance abusers is their tendency to deny their adjustment problems when they are asked to discuss them. The denial associated with their school problem is often a cover for their drinking or drug problem. With the denial, students usually promise a teacher or counselor that they can handle their own school issues and the adult does not need to worry. This optimism about changing their school performance serves to mask the underlying cause of that problem—substance abuse.

The task of detecting and dealing with students who are drug or alcohol involved is difficult and can make school staff members feel uncomfortable.

HOW SCHOOLS SHOULD DEAL WITH SUBSTANCE ABUSE ISSUES

Treatment, both administrative and therapeutic, must be aggressive. Students who abuse drugs and alcohol will not do well in school or respond to treatment of other problems until their abuse problem is treated.

School staff members have the difficult task of both enforcing the law concerning substance abuse and of breaking through the students' or families' denial of the problem. Fortunately, both tasks can be accomplished through similar means. School administrations must develop and exercise a very strict policy concerning this issue. A policy that permits second chances will only postpone an inevitable confrontation with the problem in the future. By taking immediate action with substance abusers, school staff members can help students overcome their denial. This is the first step toward helping them find treatment. The following drug policy is used in a public school in the Commonwealth of Massachusetts. It can be used as a sample of a strict drug and alcohol policy.

(1) Teachers or staff members who detect the following must immediately report to the school principal (or designee):
   —Students who demonstrate erratic or atypical behavior.
   —Students who smell of marijuana or alcohol.
   —Staff members are not responsible for determining whether or not drugs or alcohol has been used. They are responsible for providing information to their supervisors that supports why they suspect a student is involved.

(2) Administrative staff members investigate the incident according to the established practices of their school districts.

(3) Students who are found to be under the influence are suspended from school.

(4) Students who possess drugs are reported to the local police.

(5) Students who possess alcohol and who are under the legal drinking age are also referred to the local authorities.

A strict policy helps to alert the student body about the attitude the school has toward drugs and alcohol. Students must understand that the adults who teach and counsel them are strongly opposed to substance abuse. The policy demands that immediate and strong action be taken. This increases the chances of uncovering the underlying problem of substance abuse.

While a strong administrative policy can serve to identify and control drug- and alcohol-related abuses, students' overall adjustment to their problems must be addressed through comprehensive drug treatment services. Educational and therapeutic treatment services are ineffective while students are drug or alcohol dependent.[6,7] The use of drugs prevents students from experiencing the pain and stress that would otherwise motivate them to seek help. When drugs are used to alter negative or uncomfortable mental states, students suffer from the illusion that their lives are satisfactory when under their influence. It therefore appears to them that educational services or counseling is unnecessary.

Addicted students must be placed in detoxification treatment centers as an initial treatment step. Unless they are court involved, facilitating this placement may be very difficult due to denial and resistance. Teachers and counselors must work with parents to help them understand the severity of the problem. Frequently, the denial of parents undermines their capacity to deal with the problem realistically. Additional hurdles are encountered by the high cost and low availability of treatment facilities. Unfortunately, the only approach that is left in some cases is to wait until the student becomes worse. This is difficult for schools to do, but may be, by default, the only position left. Counselors should continue to advocate referral to detoxification programs during this time. They also should maintain contact with the family to help parents avoid the pitfall of believing that some less intensive intervention will solve the problem. For example, if parents believe that a change in classes or joining a club or organization will help their child with a problem of addiction, they are kidding themselves. This naive gesture to place the student in a different peer group will only work for students who have very minor problems. Addicted students require detoxification programs, and parents need to be persuaded to consider this treatment.

Parents, even with the help of competent teachers, counselors, and the agencies, will not eliminate the problem of substances abuse. School administrations must encourage teachers and counselors to remain vigilant in recognizing problems and energetic in facilitating their treatment. Individual, group, and classroom techniques must be used to provide a variety of resources of students in school, and referral to community agencies, such as Alcoholics Anonymous and Alateen should be employed. The combined effort of many people and cumulative results of various treatment options will make a difference. You are encouraged to consult the list of additional readings for both teachers and students listed at the end of the chapter.

Notes

1. S. L. Englebardt, *Kids and Alcohol, The Deadliest Drug* (New York: Lothrop, Lee & Shepard, 1975).

2. S. Cohen, *The Substance Abuse Problems* (New York: Haworth Press, 1981).

3. E. Rosenberg, *Growing Up Feeling Good: A Growing Up Handbook Especially for Kids* (New York: Beaufort Books, 1987).

4. M. Heuer, *Happy Daze* (Denver, Co.: M.A.C. Printing and Publishing Division, 1985), p. 9.

5. Ibid., p. 15.

6. Cohen, *The Substance Abuse Problems.*

7. J. Kinney, and G. Leaton, *Loosening the Grip: A Handbook of Alcohol Information* (St. Louis, Mo.; C.V. Mosby, 1978).

Additional Readings for Teachers and Counselors

Gerne, Timothy A., and Gerne, Patricia J. *Substance Abuse Prevention Activities for Elementary Children.* Englewood Cliffs, N.J.: Prentice Hall, 1986.

Schnoll, S. Getting Help: Treatments for Drug Abuse. The Encyclopedia of Psychoactive Drugs. New York: Chelsea House, 1986.

Tessler, D. J. *Drugs, Kids, and Schools: Practical Strategies for Educators and Other Concerned Adults.* Santa Monica, Calif.: Goodyear, *Publishing Company, Inc.*, 1980.

Additional Readings for Students

Hyde, Margaret, O. *Know About Alcohol.* New York: McGraw-Hill, 1978.

Hyde, Margaret, O. *Hotline.* New York: McGraw-Hill, Company, 1976.

Levinson, N., and Rocking, J., *Getting High in Natural Ways: An Infobook for Young People of All Ages.* Claremont, Calif.: Hunter House, 1986.

Miner, J. C., *Alcohol and Teens.* New York: Julian Messner, A Division of Simon & Schuster, Inc., 1984.

Rattray, J., Howells, B., and Siegler, I. *Kids and Drugs: Facts and Ideas about Using and Misusing Drugs.* Deerfield Beach, Fla.: Health Communications, 1983.

Rattray, J., Howells, B., and Siegler, I., *Kids and Alcohol: Facts and Ideas about Drinking and Not Drinking.* Deerfield Beach, Fla.: Health Communications, 1983.

14

Child Abuse and Neglect

Child abuse and neglect is an insidious plague in our society. The extent to which it exists is rapidly becoming more and more obvious. Because children pass through our schools, we are in one of the best positions to screen for situations of abuse and neglect. However, this subject is a hard one to face and an even harder one to act on. Each of us wants to believe it really is not happening. But it is. In her book *Cry Softly: The Story of Child Abuse* (Philadelphia: The Westminster Press, 1980), Margaret O. Hyde states that child abuse is the number one killer of children. She points out that child welfare experts estimate that as many as 5,000 children die each year from assaults from the adults who are responsible for caring for them. Millions more suffer from some sort of abuse. Hyde emphasizes her concern further by reporting that each day, "as many as twelve children suffer from permanent brain damage from abuse, and it is estimated that every two minutes a child is attacked by one or both parents."[1] What may be even more shocking is the increase in reported and substantiated cases each year. This is particularly true for sexual abuse. There is about a 25 percent chance that a girl will be sexually assaulted by the time she reaches early adolescence (Kinsey, quoted in Adams and Fay). The educator has a critical role in helping to treat this diseased aspect of our society.

WHAT ARE ABUSE AND NEGLECT?

The U.S. Congress defines child abuse as "the physical or mental injury, sexual abuse, negligent treatment or maltreatment of a child under the age of eighteen by a person who is responsible for the child's welfare ... ".[2]

Students can be abused by their parents or other members of their households either physically or psychologically. Physical abuse can vary from sexual abuse and harsh discipline, such as repeated spankings, to violent acts such as beatings or burnings with cigarettes. It constitutes physical harm to the child. Psychological abuse is a form of mental cruelty during which the child is repeatedly berated, harassed, threatened, or ignored. Sexual abuse can involve a combination of physical and psychological abuse. The result of this abuse is to undermine the ego and to destroy self-esteem. A child's sense of self is damaged or not permitted to develop.

Neglect is a passive kind of abuse. Students who are neglected have parents whose lives are so complicated that they are not able to provide the nurturance and care their children need. Negligence might result from a parent's being overwhelmed by his or her work or by personal problems. Parents who are substance abusers are frequently neglectful, if not abusive. These parents do not have the physical or emotional resources to attend to the emotional or physical needs of their children. As a result, these students must struggle to provide for their own physical needs, such as finding adequate food and clothing. They do not receive the time, care, and attention of the adults in their homes and frequently cannot develop substitute relationships to satisfy their needs.

Students who are abused and neglected have adjustment problems in school. It is highly unlikely that children who are being hurt by the adults who are responsible for their care will not have difficulty with the process of growing up and adjusting to school and the community. Abused and/or neglected students may show symptoms in school that will be obvious to you. But it is just as likely that their symptoms will not be obvious. The screening and identifying you do throughout your normal routines as teachers and counselors might uncover those symptoms. The list of problem behaviors in Chapter One includes characteristics that abused and neglected students often have. However, teachers and counselors must watch for specific physical and emotional signs of abuse or neglect. Bruises, cuts, burn marks, or broken bones are obvious signs of adults abusing their children. Of particular concern is the presence of a sign of physical abuse that seems to occur repeatedly and for which no clear explanation is offered. Writers in the field of child abuse provide checklists that can be summarized for use by teachers and counselors. Some of the danger signs can be directly observed by school staff members, while others can be detected by gathering information anecdotally from reports from abused students or their friends. Both kinds of indicators must be used in screening by teachers. Hyde has developed the following list of signs teachers or counselors might observe:

- Dirty clothing or unkempt appearance,
- Unexplained injuries
- Shy, withdrawn behavior; overly cooperative or eager behavior
- Reluctance to go home after school
- Wearing long sleeve shirts during warm weather
- Acting nervous or destructive, exhibiting a fear of being touched
- Unexplained absences from school
- Interpersonal problems with other students[3]

Information teachers or counselors might collect from reports of parents, other adults, or students is also important. Adams and Fay list some behaviors that should be treated as danger signs if reported:

- Sleep disturbances
- Student's not wanting to be left alone with someone
- Sudden change in appetite

- New fears or sudden need for reassurance
- Regressive or infantile behavior
- Rapid shift in behavior or mood
- Sudden alienation from one parent[4]

Both Hyde and Adams and Fay emphasize that their lists of danger signs do not necessarily indicate abuse. They are behaviors that indicate a high probability that a student is under stress and *may* be a victim of abuse.

If you question a student about an injury (or any other danger sign), as you should, and the answer you receive is confusing, you need to investigate the situation further. Immediate referral to the school nurse is necessary. A greater concern might be aroused if the student is evasive or refuses to respond to your inquiry.

Other possible indications of abuse involve the way students interact with you. A student who seems very uncomfortable alone with you or who flinches when you approach him may be a student who has been traumatized by other adults. Students who have been neglected, on the other hand, may place unrealistic demands on your time or be provocative in such a way as to engage you to give them more attention. But they also might be extremely passive and withdrawn, due to depression or physical exhaustion. Recognizing abuse and neglect may involve noticing patterns more than single events.

It is common, however, for abused or neglected students to attempt to hide their problem. This dynamic makes the subject of abuse and neglect a special subject. It deserves special attention in every school. The methods for identifying and treating problems in the previous parts of the book are all relevant. But there are additional considerations that are idiosyncratic to students who are abused and neglected. Your role as teacher or counselor is therefore also unique. You are mandated by law in most states to report any suspicion you may have that a student is either abused or neglected. At the same time you are screening for signs of abuse or neglect that the student normally feels compelled to hide from you. The position of teacher or counselor can feel very precarious as a result.

WHY ABUSED OR NEGLECTED STUDENTS ARE
HARD TO IDENTIFY

Students sometimes mask the signs of abuse or neglect to protect their families. The loyalty and devotion they feel toward their parents or caretakers is very powerful. Consequently, they can tolerate incredible amounts of abuse and neglect and continue to believe that they are to blame for the problems and would be thought of as bad by adults if they were to share their tragedy with a teacher or counselor. The guilt they experience when they contemplate telling the truth is extremely powerful.

In other cases, children fear recrimination from a particularly violent parent or caretaker, who may threaten to hurt them if they tell the family secrets. Still others may fear that the authorities will remove them from the homes and place them in foster care. A fear of abandonment is therefore another reason why many abused or neglected students hide their symptoms. Victims of sexual abuse feel guilty and ashamed about their situation in in addition to the fears just listed. They may be totally immobilized by these feelings and unable to act in any way to help change their situation. The literature on abuse and neglect is vast and worth exploring. Please refer to the references listed at end of the chapter.

TO FILE OR NOT TO FILE A PETITION OF
ABUSE OR NEGLECT

School staff members are fighting some powerful forces in an effort to help abused and neglected students. We tend to distrust our own judgment when faced with a student whom we suspect is abused. It is hard to think about this subject and easy to allow many cases to slip by us by rationalizing them in some way. We might wonder about a child and conclude that we don't have enough information to pursue the case any further. Filing a petition of suspected abuse and neglect with the state department of social services may be one of the hardest things you will ever do as a school staff member. It is easy to succumb to the temptation to believe that you were overly sensitive or overreactive, and then decide not to file. Your fear of alienating the parent is another reason for avoiding the question of whether or not to file. And, finally, many school staff members become preoccupied with the question as to whether the abuse or neglect really exists. It is extremely difficult to initiate this legal investigation if you are not sure the situation exists.

HOW TO DEAL WITH YOUR AMBIVALENCE
ABOUT FILING

You must remember that it is *not* your role to determine abuse or neglect. A social service agency, usually the state department of social services, has a team of experts who are specialists at investigating petitions of suspected abuse and neglect. It is extremely difficult to remember this, because all your time and energy is devoted to wondering if the condition exists. You do not report abuse or neglect. You report *reasonable suspicion*. The law in most states requires you to do this. (Whether your name will be kept anonymous may vary from state to state). As soon as you have reason to wonder, you must act. Take the following steps:

1. Consult your immediate supervisor. Discuss what you have observed and ask other teachers who work with the student to share any information that they may have. By involving other professionals, you share some of the burden of this difficult conflict. You also create a forum to clarify your feelings and to gather additional information.

2. If you continue to *suspect* that a student is abused or neglected, contact your local division of social services. (In some cases, your school administrator may do this for you.) Ask for the social worker who is responsible for abuse and neglect reports. Tell the worker why you are concerned and ask them to advise you accordingly. You may be asked to make an oral report only, an oral report followed by a written report, or to make a written report. Obviously, if a student appears to be in immediate danger, the social worker must act based on your telephone report, but you may be asked to follow up with a written report.

WHAT HAPPENS ONCE A REPORT IS FILED

The following sequence of steps represents an example of the process that the Commonwealth of Massachusetts follows. Your state may handle reports differently, but the social worker you contact can explain to you what you may expect.

1. The family is contacted by the investigative worker. The contact may be made immediately if the child is considered to be in immediate danger. Otherwise, contact is made as soon as possible, depending upon how busy the agency is with other reports. Usually contact is made within 24 hours.

2. The worker explains to the family that you (or, in some states, "a school teacher") have contacted them, as you are mandated to by the law, because you have information that raises the questions of either abuse or neglect in the household. The worker should point out to the family that you do not know what the situation is but once you were made aware of *(description of your concerns)*, you, as a mandated reporter, had to contact the division of social service or risk a fine. The social worker then undertakes an investigation during which additional information is gathered.

3. The agency must then decide whether or not to "substantiate" the petition you have filed. At this time, court involvement may occur, and the family may be referred to social services. There are excellent books that discuss the court process and the therapeutic services children and their family might receive.[5,6]

HOW TO SALVAGE YOUR RELATIONSHIP WITH PARENTS IF YOU FILE

It is difficult to predict how a family or student will respond to you if you file an abuse or neglect petition. Whether or not they know your specific identity, the odds are that they will be very angry and act as if you have conspired to discredit them. You may never be able to move beyond the conflict created by their outrage. What you have done "in good faith" to obey the law may unfortunately represent the end of your working relationship, if you have one. But there is a possibility that you can maintain an effective working relationship with the family.

Social workers know that, whether or not they substantiate a petition, the child will in most cases continue to have you as a teacher or counselor. They also realize that the school staff is in an excellent position to maintain an ongoing helping relationship with the student. Consequently, the investigative worker tries very hard to help the parents realize that you made a report because you had to by law once you received the information that you did. They attempt to help the parent resolve their anger and deal with their outrage. By doing this they help to preserve your relationship with the family.

In some cases parents are relieved once an investigation occurs. If a teacher, counselor, or social worker tells parents that they are in need of help for a very serious problem, it may confirm what they already know, but are afraid to admit. Being treated as someone with a problem and then helped to acquire therapy mobilizes some parents towards changing the situation in their home. They may not know how to acquire help. The child's display of symptoms in school initiates the process of the family's receiving help. It is, therefore, possible that families are grateful you have started the process.

You can also play a role in salvaging the relationship with the family, assuming you have one before you file a petition. With the approval of your administrator and the support of the social worker, you can call the parent and say the following:

"I am calling you to tell you something that I think will be very upsetting to you, but I respect you as a parent enough that I want you to hear directly from me. _____ has made these comments or _____ has shown me _____. I really don't know what these reports mean or if what _____ has said is true, but by law I am required to inform the department of social services when I hear these things. I realize this is probably very upsetting and that it may make you feel that you don't want to work with me any longer. But I am calling you to tell you that I believe we both want what is best for _____, and I hope you will feel that we can continue to work together. We need to help _____ deal with this issue as soon as possible and return our attention to helping him (her) do better in school."

You have now made a gesture to the parents to indicate that you want to continue to work with them and accept them as partners in the process of helping the child. When the parents hear how you speak to them on the telephone, it provides them with information they would not otherwise have. Without direct contact from you they will naturally imagine that you have made strong judgments about them. Reaching out by calling them can help to salvage a relationship with them. It is worth trying to do this even if the odds are small that parents will want to work with you. But you still remain the child's teacher or counselor in most cases, and must continue with the process of helping with their adjustment to school. Experts say that there is a very good chance that a problem can be treated successfully if the right therapeutic service is offered to a family. Your coordination and effort with the appropriate social service agency can make a significant difference.

We must not deny our potential role in helping to find ways to provide assistance to children who are victims of abuse and neglect. Other adjustment problems will not go away unless the sources of abuse and/or neglect are dealt with. Our efforts as educators and counselors to work directly with children who suffer from abuse is crucial. But of equal importance is the advocacy and support you provide to your school system to develop curricula that deal with the issue of abuse. Many programs involve plays, games, and tapes that have been developed for use with young children. Education at an early level can help children develop coping strategies that may help them avoid being abused or make it more likely that they can report their situation sooner to an adult who can help them. Please consult the notes at the end of the chapter for additional readings and list of agencies and hotlines concerning child abuse and neglect.

Notes

1. M. O. Hyde, *Cry Softly: The Story of Child Abuse* (Philadelphia: The Westminster Press, 1980), p. 8.

2. Ibid., p. 12.

3. Ibid., p. 28. © The Westminster Press; used by permission.

4. C. Adams and J. Fay, *No More Secrets: Protecting Your Child from Sexual Assault* (San Luis Obispo, Calif.: Impact Publishers, 1981), pp. 61–62.

5. C. K. Kempe, and R. E. Helfer eds., *Helping the Battered Child and His Family* (Philadelphia: J. B. Lippincott Company, 1972).

6. N. F. Chase, *A Child Is Being Beaten: Violence Against Children, An American Tragedy* (New York: Holt, Rinehart and Winston, 1975).

Additional Reading

Winston-Hiller, R. *Some Secrets Are for Sharing.* Denver, Colo.: MAC Printing and Publications, 1986.

Rush, F. *The Best Kept Secret: Sexual Abuse of Children.* Englewood Cliffs, N.J.: Prentice Hall, 1980.

Hotlines
Childhelp
    1-800-4-A-CHILD

National Center for Missing and Exploited Children
    1-800-621-4000

Parents Anonymous
    1-800-421-0368

Child Abuse Hot Line
    1-800-422-4453

Missing Children Help Center
    1-800-USA-KIDS

15

Attentional Deficit Hyperactivity and Disorder

Attentional deficit disorder (ADHD), (previously referred to as ADD), is a very special topic for educators, partly because it is a disorder that is widespread, but grossly under diagnosed. Diagnosis commonly depends upon descriptive information teachers and counselors give to physicians; ADHD cannot be diagnosed in a physician's office without data on how the student functions during the completion of academic tasks. The symptoms of ADHD may not be displayed unless the student is observed in a setting large enough to be fairly typical of a regular classroom, with its inherent sources of distraction. Teaching students with untreated ADHD can be extremely frustrating. They cannot respond to the normal cues you give them to correct their behavior. What works for most students seems to be almost totally ineffective for these students. It is, therefore, extremely easy to be influenced by two very limiting beliefs: first, that the student willingly and maliciously defies you to aggravate you, and, second, that you are incompetent because you cannot change their dysfunctional behavior. It's also a difficult topic, because in most cases treatment for ADHD appears to be ineffec-

tive without the use of medications. However, the use of psychotropic medications with school students is extremely controversial
in the minds of many people, particularly parents and child
advocacy groups.

ADHD is a special topic because its diagnosis and treatment
is special. Although not treating it will not, in most cases, cause
immediate and catastrophic harm to the student, the long-term
effects on students of going through school with untreated
ADHD can be very harmful. Researchers have found that children who have not received treatment for ADHD are much more
prone to become law offenders and/or substance abusers when
they grow older.[1]

ADHD is a problem that must be dealt with by all educators.
We inherit this responsibility by the fact of our proximity to
students for 180 days of the year and our ethical commitment to
furthering the healthy growth and development of our students.

WHAT IS ATTENTIONAL DEFICIT DISORDER (ADHD)?

ADHD is a disorder that results from a deficit of chemical
neurotransmitters in the brain. The purpose of these chemical
transmitters is to provide a medium through which information is
passed. Students with ADHD have a diminished capacity to do
this. Medications boost the neurotransmitters, helping students
to remain more focused. Students who can remain focused have a
greater tendency to become engrossed in their school work and
are more resistant to distractions. They look less physically active
and appear to be able to concentrate better.

HOW IS ADHD DETECTED?

In practical terms, ADHD is what a pediatrician diagnoses as
ADHD. It is a difficult task to tease apart the symptoms of
students who demonstrate ADHD-like behavior as a result of
other emotional problems from students who are thought to lack
sufficient neurotransmitters to function effectively in school.
Some of the behavior profiles described in Chapter One are
typical of cases of students who appear to be hyperactive and
inattentive, but who suffer from other emotional adjustment

problems. These may include students who are anxious, manipulative, or hostile. Pediatricians, therefore, have a challenging role as diagnosticians, and in all cases depend heavily on the reports from teachers and counselors as well as parents before they can construct a complete picture of a student's problem. Educators and parents have a particularly valuable resource in hospitals that have developmental teams that sponsor school performance evaluation programs. Evaluations are performed by a team of professionals, including a developmental pediatrician or pediatric neurologist. Chapter Nine provides a comprehensive description of a development team and the various professionals who comprise that team.

A diagnosis of ADHD usually results if the examiner eliminates other possible explanations for the symptomatic behavior that is observed during the evaluation and reported by teachers and parents. There is no medical test for ADHD. Once psychological and neurological factors are ruled out, a diagnostician depends heavily on observations made of the child in his classroom or home. Developmental teams frequently send questionnaires to classroom teachers and counselors. It can feel like an imposition to fill out these questionnaires, because some of them may take up to one hour to complete. It is conceivable that you will be asked to fill out the same form both before and during treatment.

THE TEACHER'S OR COUNSELOR'S ROLE IN DIAGNOSIS

Occasionally a physician will attempt a "trial of medication" with the classroom teacher being kept "blind." This means that a medication will be given for a brief period of time to determine if the student improves in school and to detect any possible side effects. The classroom teacher is not told of this trial period (i.e., "blind") to prevent any distortion in the report of symptoms. A situation like this, should you eventually become aware of it, is not cause for resentment. Doctors face a difficult task in identifying ADHD, and your observations are their primary source of data. If you know a student is being given a treatment involving medications, it is only natural for you to observe that student inadvertently a little more often. Once you alter the way you interact with the student, even if it is only slightly, the results of the trial medication can be influenced.

ADHD does not appear to be as serious as drug abuse or child abuse. But remember, if your student has ADHD, and it is not diagnosed and treated, there is a strong possibility that serious adjustment problems will develop in the future.

RECOGNIZING THE SIGNS OF ADHD WITH OR WITHOUT HYPERACTIVITY

Most teachers and counselors do not need a book to tell them how to recognize a "hyperactive student." Most of these students immediately find you. They engage you by wanting to know what page in the lesson you are on or if they can sharpen their pencil for the fifth time in the period. Hyperactive students identify themselves by creating such an array of distracting behaviors in the classroom that you can easily invest 90 percent of your energy on those several students. Research also indicates that there is a much higher percentage of boys diagnosed as having ADHD than girls.

ADHD can also exist without hyperactivity and can take two different forms. Recent studies of brain functioning have disclosed that some students have attentional deficits because they are overfocused. These students become so engrossed on specific details in their immediate environment that they become impervious to input from the teacher. Other students, more commonly identified as ADHD, are underfocused, and respond to so many stimuli that they cannot maintain concentration on any one detail long enough to accomplish many academic tasks successfully. Students with ADHD, with or without hyperactivity, are overfocused or underfocused, and have a serious disability. Unfortunately, they cannot derive the rewards from school that other students can. They are robbed of a sense of satisfaction from performing well and limited in their ability to develop strong motivating interests in their subject areas. Their self-esteem can become severely damaged, and the constant frustration they face can lead to the development of other symptoms such as rage reactions and depression. If you have worked in a classroom with several students with ADHD, you may have experienced the frustration of repeatedly feeling that you can almost control them, but day after day fail to do so. That can be extremely aggravating. That is the way they feel. Day after day they try and fail to gain successes. And they do try. They invest a great amount of energy into their school day. Unfortunately, much of this energy is drained off by compensatory behaviors to help them cope with what feels to them like an intolerably frustrating school situation.

A BEHAVIORAL CHECKLIST FOR ADHD SYMPTOMS

The American Psychiatric Association (APA) publishes a manual that categorizes all mental disorders. It lists behavior that characterizes students who may have ADHD (previously called ADD).

Note: Consider a criterion met only if the behavior is considerably more frequent than that of most people of the same mental age.

A. A disturbance of at least six months during which at least eight of the following are present:

1. often fidgets with hands or feet or squirms in seat (in adolescents, may be limited to subjective feelings of restlessness)

2. has difficulty remaining seated when required to do so

3. is easily distracted by extraneous stimuli

4. has difficulty awaiting turn in games or group situations

5. often blurts out answers to questions before they have been completed

6. has difficulty following through on instructions from others (not due to oppositional behavior or failure of comprehension), e.g., fails to finish chores

7. has difficulty sustaining attention in tasks or play activities

8. often shifts from one uncompleted activity to another

9. has difficulty playing quietly

10. often talks excessively

11. often interrupts or intrudes on others, e.g., butts into other children's games

12. often does not seem to listen to what is being said to him or her

13. often loses things necessary for tasks or activities at school or at home (e.g., toys, pencils, books, assignments)

14. often engages in physically dangerous activities without considering possible consequences (not for the purpose of thrill-seeking), e.g., runs into street without looking

(Note: The above items are listed in descending order of discriminating power based on data from a national field trial of the DSM-III-R criteria for Disruptive Behavior Disorders.)

B. Onset before the age of seven.

C. Does not meet the criteria for a Pervasive Developmental Disorder.[2]

If you encounter a student with behaviors that meet the APA's criteria for ADHD, a referral should be made for evaluation. Traditionally, researchers have considered ADHD to be a disorder generally affecting preadolescent children. More recent findings indicate that the effect of ADHD can persist well into adolescence and, in some cases, even into adulthood, in a residual form. However, the symptoms for adolescents may be less vivid than for children ages 8 to 10. As students grow through adolescence, they develop coping strategies and compensatory behaviors that can begin to mask their ADHD symptoms. As with other types of student adjustment problems, you are the primary source of help. Close teamwork between teachers and pediatricians is the only hope students have for timely diagnosis and treatment of ADHD.

ADHD TREATMENT AND THE CONTROVERSY SURROUNDING IT

Many experts claim that ADHD is treatable primarily through the boosting of neurotransmitters in the brain. Medications such as ritalin, cylert or benzedrine serve this function. Without medication, a student will have an extremely difficult time compensating for his or her disorder. The use of more traditional individual, group, or behavior therapies will be relatively ineffective for students with ADHD without the use of medications.

But parents and some child advocacy groups are strongly opposed to "drugging children into submission" in the classroom. They cite case studies where they believe medications have been prescribed for the wrong reasons and not properly dispensed and monitored. Consequently, some students abuse the medication and are more prone to drug abuse in later life. In a society pre-occupied with drug abuse, drug treatment for ADHD is, indeed, a controversial issue, strong enough to cause parents to storm out of a doctor's or counselor's office when medications are mentioned. It is granted that psychotropic medications have been abused, and parents have a right to be concerned about their use. But, as with any other treatment, the use of medications is neither necessarily good nor bad.

I cannot help you decide how to deal with this issue in your school system. I advise you to contact the nearest developmental evaluation team for guidance and advice. They may also be able to provide you with a list of pediatricians in your area who are known to both understand ADHD and its treatment and to work well with school teachers and counselors. I also recommend Russell A. Barkley's book, *Hyperactive Children*, as a comprehensive source of information for teachers and counselors.[3]

I deal with the issue by citing both sides of the argument to parents and strongly encouraging them to discuss treatment with their pediatrician. Meeting with a physician can provide a credible source of information to parents that school cannot do. Both the medical contraindications and the benefits of drug treatment can be discussed. This may help to dispel any fantasy parents might harbor that "the school just wants to drug my kid, because they don't know how to teach properly."

I also recommend that, if medications are used for treatment of ADHD, two additional forms of treatment be used concurrently. Medications should be thought of as a tool that can be used to help students begin to control their behavior. Highly structured school programs and counseling complete the complement of treatment components. Structure in the classroom serves as a building block for students trying to develop new behaviors. Counseling is used to educate the students about ADHD and to guide them toward developing psychological coping devices to augment the drug therapy. The counselor can serve as a case manager and maintain contact with the student's pediatrician, who should ask for regular progress reports. With the advocacy of the school counselor, the process of monitoring and adjusting medications is expedited. Physicians depend on school personnel to play this role, as they have no other direct access to the classroom process.

In summary, while most signs of ADHD and hyperactivity may be relatively easy to detect in the classroom, the process of diagnosis and treatment is, in the best of circumstances, tedious, time consuming, and possibly controversial. Living in a classroom with students with untreated ADHD is also tedious and time consuming. Advocating for evaluation and treatment is, therefore, a worthwhile investment.

Notes

1. Barkley, Russell A., *Hyperactive Children: A Handbook for Diagnosis and Treatment* (New York: The Guilford Press, 1981).

2. American Psychiatric Association, *Diagnostic and Statistical Manual of Mental Disorders,* 3rd ed., Revised (Washington, D.C.: APA, 1987), pp. 43–44. © 1980, American Psychiatric Association; used by permission.

3. Barkley, Russell A., *Hyperactive Children: A Handbook for Diagnosis and Treatment* (New York: The Guilford Press, 1981).

APPENDIX A

The Referral Process— Helping Families Find a Therapist

While a guidance staff offers counseling, there are times when families require more intensive therapeutic services. However, the transition from working with school personnel to therapists in the community can be a difficult one. Once a parent/teacher team is formed, parents may feel more comfortable continuing their relationship at school rather than involving a new person. But some adjustment problems require help outside the school. It may become necessary to add a new member(s) to the team.

Child and family therapists need the information from both parents and school. In many cases they want to work closely with the school throughout the course of treatment. This appendix outlines several aspects of a decision-making process that can be used to help parents find and utilize a therapist. While a classroom teacher will occasionally be in the position to refer parents, normally a guidance counselor or special services staff member would do this. The step-by-step decision-making process that follows represents the questions and concerns a counselor might discuss with parents who need to find a therapist in the community.

WHEN TO REFER PARENTS TO THERAPY

The following signs indicate that you need to consider referring a family for therapeutic help outside the school.

1. When all reasonable and realistic efforts have been made to help the child at home and school and the problem continues.

2. When any member of a parent/teacher team believes the child is in physical or psychological danger.

3. When parents are faced with a child who has an adjustment problem and needs the support of a family counselor.

4. When a recommendation for therapy is made from a family doctor, a member of the clergy, or an evaluation team.

THE REFERRAL PROCESS

(Please refer to section in Chapter Nine, "A Who's Who of Community Agency Professionals," for a description of the kinds of professionals who are qualified to practice psychotherapy.)

Tell parents to

1. Acquire a list of agencies or private practitioners from the school's pupil services department, your family doctor, or a member of the clergy. (If you have a list of therapists, offer them your list, but make sure you give several names.)

2. Choose several therapists form the list.

3. Call the offices of two or three therapists and inquire about

   a. Their interest or expertise in providing the kind of service you require such as

      (1) Psychological evaluation.

      (2) Individual child therapy.

      (3) Parent counseling/support.

> (4) Family therapy.
>
> b. The availability of openings.
>
> c. Fees, sliding scales, and insurance coverage.
>
> 4. Request an appointment for an initial evaluation to explain the problem and to decide how to proceed.

Tell parents that, based on the information they have gathered from their phone contact and initial evaluation session, they should be ready to choose a therapist.

WHAT THE PARENT SHOULD EXPECT DURING A PRELIMINARY EVALUATION

Explain to parents that an initial evaluation session is the time when therapists learn about their particular problem and ask them what they hope to gain from the therapy experience. Point out that they must gather enough information to make a judgment about whether or not they think they can help. Therapists may also tell you what you might expect during the term of treatment. Tell parents that it is their chance to obtain a sense of the therapist's style and personality. Emphasize that asking for an preliminary evaluation session is not synonymous with committing themselves to an ongoing long-term treatment program. It is just the first step in exploring the possibility of treatment. Ask parents to be prepared for the therapist to ask you the following:

1. Identify specific problems in clear and concise terms.
2. Be willing to talk briefly about the family history.
3. Explain what they believe the school thinks about the problem.
4. Relate what they hope for or expect from the therapy experience.
5. Think about the therapist's analysis of the problem.
6. Decide whether or not they want to schedule an appointment to begin treatment.
7. Give their permission to talk directly with the school staff who have worked with your child.

Help parents to consider carefully the therapist's recommendations even if they are different from what they expected. For example, they might believe that the treatment should involve only the child, but the therapist might believe that it could be more successful if the whole family participates.

WHAT THE PARENT SHOULD EXPECT
ONCE THERAPY BEGINS

Continue your support of parents by helping them discuss their ambivalence about the process of beginning therapy. They will frequently call you to use you as a sounding board. Do not tell them what to do or whom to see. Do point out several crucial aspects of the decision-making process to help them cope realistically with their feelings. Say to parents:

1. "If you have been or are going to be evaluated by more than one therapist, wait until you have time to think over your different experiences before you make a decision.

2. If you continue to have questions or concerns, talk them over with a friend, relative, or me at the school. You can always call the therapist to discuss your questions or even schedule one more preliminary session before you make a decision."

Providing parents still want to talk over their decision with you, continue to help them develop realistic expectations by saying that they might expect:

3. To be confused by the things the therapist wants them to do. (Therapy usually requires you to try some different behaviors that may not immediately make sense to you.)

4. To feel that things are getting worse before they are getting better. (The initial stages of therapy deal with understanding the problem more completely. As you unravel some of the issues that relate to the child's problem, you may feel that things are worse than they were before therapy began.)

5. To want to stop when things feel worse. (When you have attended several sessions and you feel worse and your child has not demonstrated immediate improvements, it is natural to want to stop. These feelings and concerns are both normal and predictable. But it is important to know what to do with them).

OR

6. To want to stop after a few sessions if things feel as though they are "all better." (There is a tendency to do this because the pressure is off, but the therapy has not taken place long enough to produce lasting changes.)

Summarize by pointing out that participation in therapy is a complex emotional process. The reactions listed only represent a few of the reactions they might have.

It is not uncommon for a family who has used you to help them find a therapist to come back to you if and when they do not want to continue with the therapy. While you cannot talk them into continuing with their therapy, you can support the process of their working with the therapist. It is predictable, when the therapy becomes intense, that they will have the impulse to quit. Parents will naturally tend to want to seek your approval for doing so. When this happens, I say the following things:

- Realize that you are beginning a difficult and painful process of trying to make things better for your child/family. It is a natural tendency to feel that you want to stop.

- Ask the therapist(s) about any issues, concerns, fears, and/or feelings that you may have. It is their job to help educate you about the process of becoming involved in and committed to the therapy process. If they don't know how you are reacting to therapy, they cannot give you the benefit of their years of training and experience to help you deal with your feelings.

- If you are satisfied with your discussion, you may have found a therapist to work with you. However, if you have diligently tried to resolve your issues by discussing your feelings and remain dissatisfied or skeptical, you may not have found a therapist to work with you! It is possible that the therapist you have started with is not the right person to help you. Part of the therapeutic experience is developing a sense of trust, openness, and commitment to the therapeutic process. Without these ingredients, the therapy will not work very well. Discuss this with the therapist(s) and decide if you want to stop. But do not forget the temptation to stop therapy because it is a difficult and painful process. You ultimately have to use your intuitive judgment as to whether or not you have found the right therapist.

You have now done what you could do to help initiate, support, and reinforce the therapy process. You may help some families overcome their resistance to a painful process. If they stop therapy, you remain a supportive resource for them. In doing so, you have also taught them a tremendous amount about the process of finding and using therapy. If their child continues to have serious adjustment problems, they may be willing to try again at a later date. If not, you have nonetheless strengthened your relationshop with them. Frequently school counselors or teachers are the only professionals parents will work with on an ongoing basis. You are therefore left the task of doing the best you can with the families of students with school and family adjustment problems.

APPENDIX B

The Conceptual Framework for Redescription

INTRODUCTION

This final section of *How to Solve Student Adjustment Problems* is presented only for the reader who is curious about the theoretical basis for redescription. You do not need to read it or to be familiar with the fairly arcane literature that supports it before you can practice redescription. But some of you may not be satisfied until you probe a little deeper and satisfy your intellectual curiosity. This is for those of you who want more than the brief introduction you received in Chapter Seven.

HISTORY

The notion of redescription grew out of ten years of clinical practice working with the families of students who have serious school adjustment problems. In my attempt to build cooperative teams with these families, I initially found that a tremendous

209

amount of time was invested in resolving conflicts. After several years it became apparent that I had to discover some way to avoid the battle before it began. The parents of students referred to me were almost always unhappy parents. They were unhappy because their children had adjustment problems that the school had not helped them with. From their point of view it is understandable why they blamed the school. However, it is difficult to work with parents who begin their relationship with you when they are angry before you have a chance to help them. Unavoidably, I began to blame them for blaming me.

Before I could help these parents, I had to find some way to overcome this "who's to blame" syndrome. With help from psychological consultants, in-service training courses, and many books and articles, I developed my strategies for redescription. They evolved as a last resort to help teachers engage parents who appear to be unengageable and, ultimately, to help deliver services to students with serious school and family adjustment problems.

In your roles as counselors or teachers, it is unlikely that you will face conflicts with large numbers of parents at one time, as I did in our clinical education program. But you will face angry parents from time to time who may blame you for their child's problem. The materials presented in Chapter Seven provide a variety of resources for working with parents in conflict situations. The following theoretical discussion is a supplement to Chapter Seven. As such, it traces the conceptual basis of redescription to its source in the literature: the relationship between neurology and language. While some of the concepts are illusive and novel, they explain why redescription works. It is a powerful thinking tool that will enhance any educator's understanding of how language can be used to reduce unhealthy conflict situations between parents and school staff members.

Two terms, "redescription" and "subculture," presented in Chapter Seven are reviewed here:

> *Redescription*: a process of using language in such a manner as to come to appreciate, respect, and account for the subculture (point of view) of other persons; this may produce different perceptions of these persons.

Subculture: the particular point of view or "idiosyncracies of perception" of any describer; that which constitutes one's way of looking at and perceiving events.

The use of redescription as a tool to resolve conflicts between people is based on the work of the neurobiologists Maturana and Varela and their study of cognition.[1,2] They discuss how an observer sees and then describes events. Redescription permits you to shift from stagnation or conflict to another level of interaction. This developmental shift can be influenced by the following:

1. Our willingness to confront the possibility that there are many ways to experience an interaction between people.
2. Our ability to employ language in such a way as to influence our experience of reality.

LANGUAGE DETERMINES WHAT
WE EXPERIENCE

A primary thesis is that we can have *language-determined experiences.* The language you use can determine what you believe about something. The description your formulate in your mind and the act of stating that description to another person can determine what you feel, believe, and experience.

I am, therefore, suggesting that there is such a thing as a perceiver-constructed reality—a language-influenced reality. As the observer constructs an experience of reality and communicates this experience to another person, a mingling of perceptions occurs, allowing each party the possibility of having a different experience of one another. For example, referring to an aggressive person as "energetic and committed," may change the way that person treats you, therefore diminishing your experience of him or her as being "aggressive."

When language is organized into a description, a spontaneous and instantaneous sequence of messages is transmitted back and forth between parties. Each party is affected simultaneously. Consequently, an experience of mutual multiple versions of reality is produced between observers. Once confronted with the phenomenon of "no objective reality," the observer is discouraged from indulging in the illusion that his or her perception of reality/phenomena is "correct." Our perceptions are only a version of reality.

However, if our version of events appears to be rigid, it can trigger resistance by constituting a threat to an individual's identity. This has implications for both educator and therapist.

WHY REDESCRIPTION IS NOT STRICTLY A THERAPIST'S TOOL

A paper by Alexander Blount provides a good starting point for understanding how our descriptions of phenomena influence our experience of reality.[3] In writing about the affective experience of the therapist, Blount states that as a therapist attempts to change the meaning of a behavior in a family session by "reframing,"[4] the therapist himself can have the experience of believing the new meaning implied by the reframing.

For example, a parent who is dominating a family interview and not allowing anyone else to speak might be described as "committed" to trying her hardest to making the family session work as opposed to being described as "domineering." As the therapist feeds back this description to the parent, she may feel a sense of relief that someone appreciates what she is trying to do and understands how worried she is. Having been satisfied that her "message" has been understood, the parent may relax the drive to dominate the session, thus allowing the therapist and other members to take a more active part. If the therapist feels more relaxed and in control of the session, the parent may in turn relax even more.

This change to a new experience is contingent upon the therapist's observation of behavior and his or her description of that behavior. The description helps to determine the reality being experienced which cues the person being described to act differently. This continually gives the person doing the describing a different set of considerations to react to and to describe and so on and so forth.

Blount's portrayal of the observer or "context"-determined experience has implications for anyone struggling to solve a conflict, particularly for teachers and counselors in school systems. While Blount speaks from the frame of reference of a family therapist, what he implies need not be limited to the therapist/client relationship. He points us in the direction of realizing that what we experience as our reality is not fixed and is contingent upon our stance as observers.

Blount's "affective experience of the therapist" is a fundamental and ever-present element in *all* human interaction, even when it differs in several fundamental ways from the therapist/client relationship. More specifically, the therapeutic technique referred to as "reframing," while similar, is not identical to redescription. Redescription has three fundamental distinctions:

1. It does not assume a therapeutic contract with an inherent distinction between therapist and client. Consequently, it does not assume one person or the other to be in a helping role, to have a greater degree of expertise in helping, or to be motivated toward interaction beyond reciprocal need. Therefore, redescription occurs between partners equally motivated to engage one another for the purpose of mutual effort toward interaction.

2. Redescription does not suggest that the describer assign a positive connotation to the new meaning that is rendered, as is often practiced in the therapeutic art of reframing.

3. Redescription is to be thought of as an ongoing incremental process of creating alternative descriptions of events; this may or may not be characteristic of reframing, depending upon how it is conceived by the therapist.

Redescription is characteristic of human interaction and is a phenomenon inclusive of reframing, while not restricted as a strictly therapeutic tool. This brings us to two fundamental questions:

How does redescription affect the way we try to change our interactions?

What characterizes one description from another relative to its potential to facilitate growth in the way we interact?

These questions are addressed by Maturana and Varela through their explanatory discussion of the biology of cognition.[5]

WHAT INFLUENCES OUR PERCEPTION OF EVENTS?

The Chilean neurobiologist Humberto Maturana and his colleague Francisco Varela, through their study of the biology of cognition, have demonstrated that what one sees depends more upon the status of the neural apparatus of the brain of the perceiver than the characteristics of the object being viewed.[6] They provide an exhaustive argument that we see what our neurological makeup predisposes us to see, and we are subject only to a subjective experience.

> Yet, for the operation of the nervous system (and organism), there cannot be a distinction between illusions, hallucinations, or perceptions, because a closed neuronal network cannot discriminate between internally and externally triggered changes in relative neuronal activity.[7]
>
> As a consequence, the human cognitive domain, the human domain of descriptions, is necessarily closed: every human assertion implies an interaction.[8]

Given the premise that we see what we are ready to see and that our experience is therefore "observer-contingent," we are compelled to realize that every phenomenon we describe can legitimately be described differently. This way of thinking is characterized by a circular interaction between two describers. Now each episode of description (as delivered through our language) triggers a different experience of reality and a different set of possibilities from which to formulate description. Our mental formulation of description is how we come to "know" another person. But this is an ongoing process of changing perceptions and reactions; it is never fixed. One can think of this as unraveling or disclosing another person's being, but only through *our* experience of their being—through *our* perceptual perspective.

The mingling of these perspectives is a mixing of our perceptual subcultures. Each individual has a particular experiential point of view which is determined not only by all the things we commonly consider cultural (race, creed, heritage, etc.) but also by the particular manner in which we collect and process information. This can be thought of as a kind of "perceptual subculture" and allows each individual to see things in a manner that is uniquely his or hers. As language is used to restate an experience of another person, a mental description is formulated. When two people interact and formulate descriptions, a process of cross-cultural interaction takes place between the describers.

What then is the effect of redescription in the realm of human affairs and how can language be used to facilitate growth toward acceptance of "subcultural differences?"

CHANGING THE WAY WE TRY TO CHANGE: SECOND-ORDER CHANGE

Hierarchical orders of class, levels of learning, and change have been discussed in a variety of ways by Blount, Bateson, and Keeney.[9,10,11] Second-order change is a change in the way we try to facilitate change. It represents a change in the possibilities of a relationship or in the set of conditions experienced by change agents. It involves second-order learning or learning how to learn, as opposed to just learning by rote memory.[12]

The constant interplay of perceptual subcultures involved in the process of redescription may contribute to an appreciation of each other's subculture. The resulting cross-cultural understanding that is an excellent example of second-order change.

SUSPENDING OUR JUDGMENT ABOUT WHAT WE BELIEVE TO BE "TRUE"

Redescription permits a flexible interaction between parties and frees a natural flow of events to drift to a new level of relationship. Redescription constantly confirms that "this is not the only experience of reality available," which opens the door to other possibilities of flexible interaction and integration. On the other hand, indulging in the illusion that your experience of reality at the moment is a "correct" reality may lead to rigidity. If the person being described has a different experience of themselves, your description may lead to a loss of face for him or her and threaten his or her identity, which can provoke resistance and conflict.

REDESCRIPTION AND THE RESOLUTION OF CONFLICT

How then, do you participate in interactions in such a manner as to enhance flexible growth toward different levels of relating?

Description that confirms the identity of a system (either individual person or larger system) will trigger second-order change with consequent metamorphosis toward another state of relationship. Any variation from the original involuntary construction of a description (with its illusion of being a "correct" description, an "objective" reality) sets the stage for redescription and "second-order change." The mere acknowledgment in the observer of other possibilities produces a better set of conditions for

> *second-order description*
>> leading to
>
> *modification of perceived realities*
>> leading to
>
> *change in experience*
>> leading to
>
> *change in description*
>> leading to
>
> *movement toward a new identity*
>> leading to
>
> *increase in possibility of different behavior*

A relationship may evolve to a new plateau as determined by the new descriptions, which free parties to alter their identity without loss of face.

IN SUMMARY

Redescription is the art of creating alternative sets of meanings. It is an invitation to let go of one's spontaneous, observer-determined descriptions for *any* alternative description. Meaning begins the moment the observer embraces the realization that "what I see is a product of my mind" and that other possibilities exist. The creative forging of meanings continues with a detailed analysis of an interaction, and follows with a regrouping or synthesis of these details into a *redescription*—a new message— with a new meaning. The analysis and synthesis of elements of description into new sets of meanings constitute the art of redescription.

This process frees parties to mutually accept one another's subculture, a process which would otherwise be inhibited by the belief in an objective reality. The confirmation of identity and enhancing of "face" permits shifts to different levels of relationship.

Notes

1. Humberto R. Maturana and Francisco J. Varela, *Autopoiesis and Cognition: The Realization of the Living* (New York: D. Reidel, 1980).

2. Humberto R. Maturana, "Biology of Language: The Epistemology of Reality," in G. A. Miller and E. Lenneberg, (eds.), *Psychology and Biology of Language and Thought: Essays in Honor of Eric Lenneberg* (New York: Academic Press, 1978).

3. Alexander Blount, "Strategic Therapy and the Affective Experience of the Therapist," *The Journal of Strategic and Systemic Therapies*, 1(3) (1982).

4. P. Watlawick, J. Weakland, and R. Fisch, *Change: Principals of Problem Formation and Problem Resolution* (New York: W. W. Norton, 1974).

5. Humberto R. Maturana, "Biology of Language: The Epistemology of Reality," in Miller and Lenneberg, (eds.), *Psychology and Biology of Language and Thought: Essays in Honor of Eric Lenneberg* (New York: Academic Press), 1978.

6. Ibid.

7. Ibid., p. 46.

8. Ibid., p. 57. © 1978, Academic Press; used by permission.

9. Blount, "Strategic Therapy and the Affective Experience of the Therapist." *The Journal of Strategic and Systemic Therapies*, 1, 3, 1982.

10. Gregory Bateson, *Mind and Nature* (New York: E.P. Dutton, 1979).

11. Bradford P. Keeney, *Aesthetics of Change* (New York: The Guilford Press, 1983).

12. Bateson, *Mind and Nature*

General Recommended Readings

Herzfeld, Gerald and Powell, Robin. *Coping for Kids: A Complete Stress Control Program for Students Ages 8–18.* (New Nyack, N.Y.: The Center for Applied Research in Education, 1986).

Hitchner, K. W., and Tifft-Hitchner, A. *A Survival Guide for the Secondary School Counselor.* (West Nyack, N.Y.: The Center for Applied Research in Education, 1987).

Medeiros, D. C., and Porter, B. J. *Children Under Stress: How to Help with the Everyday Stresses of Childhood.* (Englewood Cliffs, N.J.: Prentice Hall, 1974).

Sprick, Randall S. *Discipline in the Secondary Classroom: A Problem by Problem Survival Guide.* (West Nyack, N.Y.: The Center for Applied Research in Education, 1985).

Sulzer-Azaroff, Beth, and Mayer, G. Roy. *Applying Behavior-Analysis Procedures with Children and Youth.* (New York: Holt, Rinehart and Winston, 1977).

Index

A

Absenteeism, 10–11
  role of attendance officer, 111
Abuse, alcohol (see Alcohol Abuse)
Abuse, child abuse, 185–93
  checklist of symptoms, 27, 187–88
  defined, 186
  filing a petition, 189–91
  helping families of children, 191–93
  identification of abused children, 189
  of other students, 10–11
  when to refer, 31, 189–90
Abuse, drugs (see Drug Abuse)
ADHD (attentional deficit hyperactivity
    disorder)
  checklists, 23, 199–201
  classroom implications, 195, 202
  defined, 196
  detecting symptoms, 196–200
  evaluations, 123
  impulsivity, 8
  medication, 196–97, 200–202
  special education, 146
  treatment, 200–202
    controversy with medications,
      200–201
Adjustment counselor, 110
Adjustment problems:
  abused and neglected children, 186–87
  ADHD as a cause, 196, 198
  checklist of symptoms (see Checklist)
  drug and alcohol abuse, (see Drug,
    abuse; Alcohol, abuse)
  role of guidance counselor, 113
  screening by specialist, 143
  special education, 146
  substance abusers, 182–83
Advocating for children, 32
  ADHD, treatment controversy,
    200–202

children with special needs, 141, 151
Alateen, 183
Alcohol abuse:
  ADHD, 179
  contribution factors, 178–79
  definition of, 177
  signs of, 180–81
    guidance counselor's role, 113
  schools, role in treatment, 181–83
  treatment, 121–22, 127
Alcoholics Anonymous, 183
American Psychiatric Association, 199
Anger, resolving feelings, 99–100
Antisocial behavior, 11
  checklist, 24
Anxious students,
  checklist, 24
  description of behavior, 10
Assessments (see Evaluations)
Attendance officer, 111, 132
Attending school, 131–32
Attention deficit hyperactivity disorder
  (see ADHD)

B

Behavior, defining, 21–27
  special education, 146
  teacher's role, 165
Behaviors indicating problems, 8–12, 146
  antisocial, 11
  anxiety, 10
  depression, 10 (see also Depression)
  hostility, 10
  impulsivity, 8 (see also Impulsivity,
    ADHD)
  manipulative personality, 9
  passive-aggressive, 9
  phobia, 11